THE COMPLETE KETO COOKBOOK

AND

LIFESTYLE GUIDE

THE COMPLETE KETO COOKBOOK

AND

LIFESTYLE GUIDE

PETE EVANS

plum. Pan Macmillan Australia

CONTENTS

This book is dedicated to all the courageous people who acknowledge that real, sustainable health must always begin with the desire to learn and sometimes even challenge their own and others' beliefs. I believe that true intelligence is about being able to look at evidence that may contradict your own ideas and allowing for the possibility that you may be wrong. I wish you all the very best on your journey to discover what works best for YOU. xo

INTRODUCTION

Hello dear friends.

Thank you for picking up this book and choosing to prioritise your health by embracing nourishing wholefoods. I know that many of you have been on this journey with me over the course of the last decade and I would like to thank you for your trust and for continuing to cook and enjoy the healthy recipes I share. For those of you who are new to my work, I hope you find inspiration within these pages. I feel excited for the positive changes that are to come in your journey to better health.

The Complete Keto Cookbook and Lifestyle Guide is a comprehensive guide to the ketogenic diet and will provide all the information you'll need to understand why this diet works so well and to easily implement it in your own life. I also share lots of wonderful family-friendly recipes that will fill you with energy and vitality, and allow you to live the life you have always dreamed of.

If you are new to the keto diet, in a nutshell it is about embracing wholefoods and eating a diet that is lower in carbs and higher in healthy fats. This allows your body to switch on its ability to burn fat for fuel. Once we have trained our body to do this, we have an almost unlimited supply of energy, because instead of relying on our next meal, our body can use fat stores to create energy. This is why, once people have transitioned to this low-carb way of eating, they find they have more sustained energy throughout the day, without the highs and lows that can occur on a high-carb, low-fat diet.

I follow a paleo version of the ketogenic diet, and have been eating this way for the last decade or so. This means steering clear of foods that can cause inflammation, namely grains, legumes and dairy. Instead, I enjoy good-quality proteins and fats from well-sourced land and sea animals, as well as lots of low-carb veggies, fermented foods and bone broths. My approach is an intuitive one, in which I listen to my body and cycle in and out of a mild state of ketosis.

I do not have all the answers, but what I do know for sure is how much embracing wholefoods and a paleo-based keto approach has helped me, my family and so many of you. Two of the biggest benefits for me have been the increase in my energy levels and improved cognitive function. I love the improved clarity of thought, recall and focus that I experience through embracing this way of eating.

We are also seeing more studies emerging, which show the potential benefits of a ketogenic diet. It is possible that it may be able to help with a range of conditions, such as Alzheimer's, Parkinson's, diabetes and metabolic disorders. This book includes the most up-to-date research that I am aware of, though no doubt our understanding of how the keto diet works will continue to grow and change in years to come.

While I'm not claiming that eating keto can solve everything, I believe there are many modern-day health issues that it has the potential to help with. My intention is to channel the best nutritional information we have into a collection of delicious recipes that will help you to thrive. And while nutrition plays a major role in creating sustainable health, it's also important to work on other factors, such as sleep, mindfulness, breathwork, functional movement, play and connection to nature, as well as to try to reduce stress, negative belief patterns and environmental toxins. My dream is that we can collectively usher in a new normal in terms of the way we eat and live, where robust health is the norm rather than a rarity.

I invite you to step outside your comfort zone and try some new ingredients when cooking from this book. I believe that when you face your fears, the whole world opens up and becomes more exciting. So, if you see a recipe that features something you've never eaten, such as liver or an exotic spice, stop and ask yourself, 'What would happen if I confronted this fear and tried something new? If I can do this, what else can I face?' We all have the power to transform our own lives and that of our community simply through leading by example, and the best way we can do that is with vibrant, powerful and robust health.

Anyway, that is enough from me – it's time to get stuck into some delicious food! I invite you to open your heart, your mind and your tastebuds to what awaits on the following pages.

Cook for life with love and laughter.

PETE xo

WHY CHOOSE KETO?

WHAT IS THE KETO DIET?

In a nutshell, the ketogenic diet is a higher fat, lower carb, moderate-protein eating plan that's often combined with fasting. It was designed to free our metabolism from its dependence on sugar (glucose) and instead force our body to use fat, a more reliable source of energy that we have stored in abundance. This state of switching from burning glucose to burning fat is known as ketosis.

HOW DOES IT WORK?

Well, here goes . . . The body has two main sources of energy: glucose and fat. When we deprive our body of glucose, or abstain from food completely, we only have so long before the glucose levels fail to keep up with the voracious appetite of our brain. When the brain's energy demands exceed glucose supplies, it calls on fat for back up. But not just fat – ketones.

Ketones, a product of fat metabolism, are made by the liver when the body clues in that glucose stores are low and the brain needs an alternative energy source. You see, the brain is unlike the rest of the body as it can't use fat directly as fuel. This situation presented human evolution with one of two options:

- Break down muscle mass to turn amino acids into glucose, or
- Turn fat into ketones, a form of energy the brain could use.

Obviously, natural selection opted for the latter – saving the human race from wasting away in times of food scarcity. Evolution deserves some credit here as the reality is early primitive humans were faced with long periods without food when storing energy as body fat became crucial for survival.

In the event of a failed hunt or the limited ability to gather edible nuts, seeds and vegetation, our ancestors' body fat fuelled them as they continued on their constant quest for food. This ability to store fat is in stark contrast to glucose, which we have limited capacity to store. Depending on glucose became more or less unreliable, and that is how the situation remains to this day. Speaking in terms of evolution, humans are absolutely primed and prepared to run on fats and ketones, and many ancestral diets were ketogenic before keto even became a word.

Fast forward to the twentieth century and the early 1900s and the keto diet was developed by doctors as a treatment for childhood epilepsy.[1] Today, it is used not only as a way to burn body fat and lose weight but also to help manage medical conditions such as many of the metabolic and inflammatory disorders that, unfortunately, seem to be so much a part of modern life.

What happens when we eat carbohydrates?

As I've mentioned, our body runs on one of two primary fuels: glucose or fat.

In terms of what we eat, glucose comes from carbohydrates and fat comes from, well, fat. Carbohydrates come in many forms, such as simple sugars or complex carbs, but, at the end of the day, all carbohydrates turn to glucose in the body, with the exception of fibre (see box below for more info).

HOW IS FIBRE USED IN OUR BODY?

Fibre is technically a carbohydrate but is not fully broken down during digestion and can pass through our digestive tract without being fully absorbed. It is divided into two categories: soluble and insoluble. Soluble fibre, primarily found in fruits and legumes, is fermented in the gut, producing short-chain fatty acids that the cells lining our colon can use as fuel. Insoluble fibre, found predominantly in non-starchy vegetables (such as broccoli, eggplant and mushrooms), is the type that passes through digestion relatively unchanged.

Once glucose is in the blood, our pancreas releases insulin to shuttle glucose into cells to be used immediately as fuel, stored away as glycogen for later use, or stored as fat if the former two options are exhausted. This tightly regulated system of removing glucose from the blood is designed to maintain healthy blood sugar levels, because too much sugar in the blood for too long has the potential to cause damage.

Unfortunately, in our modern food environment (with its overconsumption of processed carbohydrates) this system is often abused, causing our cells to stop responding to insulin as well as they should. When this occurs, the pancreas has to work harder to keep producing and releasing insulin to make sure healthy blood glucose levels are maintained. Over time this well-oiled machine can break down, the pancreas can become overwhelmed by having to work so hard, increasing the risk of insulin resistance (aka prediabetes).

Remember when I mentioned that the keto diet can free our metabolism from being dependent on sugar? Processed sugars and grains release glucose rapidly into your system, spiking blood glucose to very high levels in a short amount of time. Often in this case, insulin overcompensates for the rise in blood glucose and too much is released, bringing blood glucose levels lower than they were before you ate. Just as high blood glucose can be dangerous, so too can low blood glucose. When blood glucose drops without the metabolic flexibility to tap into an alternative fuel source (fat and ketones) the brain responds by saying, 'Hey, you need to eat now, we have no fuel' and can trigger cravings for more sugar. In this way, you become quite literally a slave to sugar. Stabilising blood glucose levels with a keto diet helps beat these cravings and, at the same time, takes a major burden off your pancreas.

Reduce carbohydrates
and increase fats.
Glucose stores
become depleted.

Fatty acids released
from fat stores.

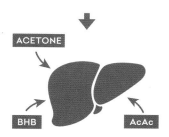

Fatty acids broken
down in liver to ketones.

Ketones replace
glucose to provide
sustained energy.

What is ketosis?

If carbohydrates are kept low enough, fat can be turned into ketones. These ketones are the result of suppressing the hormone insulin. We can lower insulin by restricting carbohydrates (and to some extent protein) or by avoiding food altogether and fasting. Low insulin allows fatty acids to be sent to the liver to be broken down for fuel and if sustained for long enough, converted to ketones. Ketones are then sent from the liver to fuel other organs such as the brain and heart. Many other organs can run on fat directly and prefer this even in a state of ketosis. Ketones and fat are metabolised in our cells to support our bodies' energy systems.

When the body produces ketones, this state is known as ketosis. Ketosis brought about while on a keto diet is referred to as nutritional ketosis, in contrast to fasting ketosis, which is induced by fasting. The main difference between the two types is:

- in a state of nutritional ketosis, the fats converted to ketones come from a combination of fat in the diet and, depending on how many calories you consume, body fat
- in a state of fasting ketosis, the fats converted to ketones come entirely from body fat stores.

THREE PRIMARY KETONES

When you are in ketosis, the liver produces three main ketones:

Beta-hydroxybutyrate (BHB) – found in greatest abundance in the body.

Acetoacetate (AcAc) – what our cells use for fuel and is produced when BHB is broken down.

Acetone – the least abundant, is created when AcAc breaks down and is excreted through the breath and urine.

For a long time, these ketones got a bad rap. They were misunderstood as metabolic waste products and worse, were labelled as dangerous when caught at the scene of the crime of diabetic ketoacidosis. Ketoacidosis, a serious metabolic state that can occur in people with type 1 diabetes, is a condition that can arise when ketones reach exceedingly high levels in the blood.

Within the last few decades, however, ketones have been seen in a different light. On countless occasions we've seen how they are anything but dangerous and, in fact, can be incredibly therapeutic.

WHAT ARE THE BENEFITS OF GOING KETO?

Going keto offers a wide range of health benefits beyond impressive control over your blood glucose levels and supplying you with the sustained energy you need to be productive and focused throughout your day. As research advances, the advantages of a keto diet have extended from treating epilepsy to various metabolic disorders, and the list continues to grow.

But how could one single diet help with so many different problems?

A common theme with many modern health issues is poorly functioning metabolism (aka metabolic dysfunction), which, more often than not, is linked to impaired glucose metabolism. Some health practitioners believe this could be the root cause of many ailments. That's because every process in your body runs on an energy system, so if your energy system is broken, problems are more likely to occur. This may explain why metabolic dysfunction and insulin resistance[2] have been linked to conditions including type 2 diabetes,[3] obesity,[4] chronic inflammation,[5] migraine,[6] polycystic ovary syndrome (PCOS),[7] certain cancers,[8] cardiovascular disease[9] and a number of neurodegenerative disorders such as Alzheimer's disease.[10]

Because the keto diet helps train the body to run on fat and ketones, it gives the body and pancreas a break from having to constantly deal with burning and storing glucose. I will never claim that keto will cure all your health issues, but I will say that it might help get to the root of many of your problems. I say this based on research that shows keto's potential to improve insulin sensitivity, lower inflammation and promote metabolic flexibility – all of which may be associated in one way or another with many chronic diseases.[11]

So, if you are interested in life-long health, removing the burden of excess sugar may be a good place to start; and training your body to run on fat may be the next step.

THE KETO DIET MAY BE ABLE TO HELP YOU ACHIEVE:

- Balanced hormonal health
- Effortless weight loss
- Improved mental clarity and focus
- Improved metabolism
- Long-lasting energy
- Improved sleep and mood
- Reduced appetite and decreased cravings
- Reduced risk of chronic diseases.

Your brain on ketones

The impact ketones have on the brain deserves its own section because the truth is the brain loves ketones! It's the reason we make ketones in the first place: to fill the role as the brain's primary fuel source when glucose isn't fitting the bill. Current research looks at the impact the keto diet and ketone supplements have on Alzheimer's disease, migraine, Parkinson's disease, epilepsy (and many other seizure disorders), brain cancer, traumatic brain injury (TBI), multiple sclerosis (MS), depression, anxiety and many other neurological disorders.[12, 13, 14, 15] This suggests something is altered in the brain when ketones become available. Understanding how vulnerable the brain is to changes in fuel availability will help us understand how ketones can benefit the brain.

Despite accounting for only about 2 per cent of the body by weight, the brain sucks up almost a quarter of our daily energy requirements.[16] To add to this, it requires that its flow of energy is constant or else brain function is compromised. In other words, the brain responds to even the slightest of glitches. With this knowledge, you can understand how constantly fluctuating blood glucose levels may have an impact. If they are either too low (hypoglycaemia) or too high (hyperglycaemia), mood, appetite and focus are affected. You might even lose the ability to think straight.

Ketones are the brain's only significant alternative fuel and can circumvent a lot of these issues by:

- preventing high blood glucose due to the low-carb nature of the diet
- providing a reliable alternative fuel when blood glucose levels are low.

TESTIMONIAL

When I was about 23 years old I gained a little weight while travelling. I used the low-fat approach to lose weight and developed a severe binge-eating habit. I was always starving and my usual great mental health took a dive, as I didn't feel like I could control myself. My mum had just discovered the keto diet and shared her recipe books with me. When I started following a keto diet with paleo principles, I found that my meals were finally satisfying, so I was no longer thinking about food every second! The weight came off on its own, I had more energy and my inflamed skin cleared up. I'm a shift worker in a high-stress job and this way of eating has given me more mental clarity and satisfies me so that I don't feel the temptation to give into fast food when there's no time for anything else. The keto diet has changed my life, and I've inspired some family and friends to get on board too.

Michaela, 29 years

As I've already mentioned, when you are in a state of ketosis, you have access to infinite fuel – fat in the form of ketones – which means a constant supply to the brain that doesn't depend on how often you eat. Essentially, you're wearing your next meal!

But the benefits go beyond sustained energy and, as we age, ketones may offer the brain protective armour. It is not uncommon for the brain to lose its ability to properly use glucose as we grow older.[17] So, even as you continue to put fuel in the form of carbohydrates into your body, the brain doesn't receive it. Without an alternative fuel (ketones), the health of your brain may decline, since energy fuels your brain's reparative and restorative processes. Research has shown that brain glucose metabolism can start slowing down decades before any symptoms of cognitive decline are noticed.[18] And, unsurprisingly, a hallmark of Alzheimer's disease is reduced brain glucose metabolism.

However, the brain's ability to take in and turn ketones into energy doesn't seem to deteriorate with age. It's possible that ketones protect the brain. At this stage it's only a theory but it may turn out that throughout your life occasionally exposing your brain to ketones could be a way to delay or prevent you losing your mind, so to speak.

Other potential benefits of ketones include reduced inflammation and improved protection of the brain, greater cognitive function, an increase in a feeling of wellbeing[19] and to top it all off they may slow the ageing process.

So, ketones:

- provide a constant source of energy to the brain, helping to prevent the negative impact of fluctuating blood glucose levels
- are a reliable source of fuel for the brain and may be able to help overcome health issues as we age, potentially protecting the brain from degeneration and diseases like dementia
- may lower inflammation in the brain
- may reduce stress-induced damage
- can have a calming effect.

WRONGFULLY VILIFYING FAT

If you first scoffed at the idea of a keto diet because there was no way an eating plan based on fat could be healthy, you're not alone. The keto diet receives a lot of criticism from those who don't think that fat is, in fact, part of a healthy diet. We have all heard that fat, particularly saturated fat, can cause heart disease, but what if we end up discovering that fat is not the villain it's been made out to be?

How did the low-fat diet end up being touted as the way to eat?

Well, at the beginning of the 1970s a low-fat diet was adopted by most of the Westernised world, largely based on early (and flawed) research showing a correlation between high-fat diets, high cholesterol levels and higher rates of heart disease. From this the diet–heart hypothesis was born, claiming that fat in the diet = cholesterol in the blood = heart disease. In response, to reduce the risk of heart disease, a low-fat diet was prescribed; it was also promoted for weight loss. Ironically, the advice to reduce dietary fat parallels nicely with the increased rates of obesity and type 2 diabetes, possibly due to fat being replaced with refined carbohydrates. Cereals, crackers, pasta and bread may be low in fat but that doesn't mean they aren't fattening.

The low-fat trend sank its teeth into the politics of food and had a strong influence on governmental dietary guidelines worldwide. The low-fat diet was everywhere. Cardiovascular risk factors seemingly dropped for most and deaths from heart disease fell substantially. Success! Wait, not so fast. Although mortality from heart disease fell, incidences of heart disease did not.[20] People were getting fatter and sicker – and were living longer while fat and sick. Attempts to validate the diet–heart hypothesis have failed to show cause and effect, and more and more research demonstrates that reducing dietary fat and, more specifically, saturated fat does not translate to reduced risk of heart disease.[21]

What we can take away from this is that fat is innocent until proven guilty and context matters. What you eat with your fat, the quality and source of your fat and a whole range of lifestyle factors must also be considered. The theory that dietary fat causes heart disease still remains a hypothesis today, despite some studies casting doubt on it.[22] I should also note here that ketogenic studies have shown high-fat, low-carb diets improve markers of cardiovascular disease risk.[23]

DIFFERENT KETO APPROACHES

Since it was first introduced in the 1920s, the keto diet has evolved to include a number of variations that make sticking to this way of eating much easier. If you are new to all this and want to know what it feels like to be in ketosis, I recommend starting with a restrictive keto diet (see Classic Keto and Modified Keto, below) before adopting an intuitive approach (more on this to come). Giving your body a period to become keto adapted while going through the initial transition from being a sugar burner to a fat burner makes it easier for your metabolism to cycle in and out of ketosis. After you've introduced your body to ketosis and given it time to adapt, you can experiment with different approaches based on your preference, intuition and lifestyle (remember, that's important!). Keeping a food diary can help with finding what works best for you. Jot down what you're eating and how you're feeling afterwards until you get your bearings.

Classic keto

The first keto diet ever clinically studied was given the name 'classic ketogenic diet'. It's also referred to as the 4:1 ketogenic diet, describing 4 parts fat to 1 part carbs plus protein. This roughly translates to getting 90 per cent of calories from fat, 6–10 per cent from protein and 0–4 per cent from carbohydrates. This very fat-heavy keto eating plan is almost foolproof for entering ketosis and is ideal if you want to stay in a constant state of ketosis; however, it's also the most restrictive. This approach is mostly followed by people with chronic illness, and it severely limits what you can eat. Although it isn't for most people, you might like to start out on a classic keto diet to help familiarise yourself with what it's like to be in ketosis and to see how your body reacts. The downsides are that this approach can be difficult to stick to long term and you may find you experience many of the symptoms associated with 'keto flu' (see page 28).

Modified keto

Modified versions of the keto diet include more protein and slightly more carbs and are less restrictive than a classic keto diet. These variations still allow you to achieve ketosis, just without having to stick to such a stringent eating plan. Most people will go into ketosis if they keep total carbs under 50 grams per day and protein within the range of 1.5–1.8 grams per kilogram of body weight. Fat provides the rest of your energy needs, which you are usually advised to eat until you feel full. For a modified keto diet, 65–85 per cent of your calories come from fat, 15–35 per cent come from protein and 0–10 per cent come from carbs. It's important to remember your carbs need to come from nutrient-dense, high-fibre, plant-based foods and low-glycaemic vegetables (think leafy greens, asparagus, cucumber and cauliflower), nuts and seeds. A modified keto diet is much easier to stick to. So, for example, if your day revolves around eating under 30 grams of carbs but it's creating stress in your life and upping that to 50 grams makes the diet work for you (at the expense of lower ketone levels), opt for the latter.

Cyclical keto

The cyclical keto approach uses carbs in a strategic way to intentionally cycle in and out of ketosis. This requires you to first enter ketosis using a stringent keto eating plan that limits carbs to under 50 grams per day. You then break out of ketosis by reintroducing anywhere from 50 to 150 grams of carbs for one day every week, fortnight or month. This isn't meant to be a day to go completely bananas on carbs (pun intended), the purpose is more to mimic ancestral hunter–gatherer patterns where carbs would have been eaten only when accessible. Your carbs should ideally come from nutrient-dense wholefoods and starchy root vegetables (like sweet potato or pumpkin), not from processed grains or sugars that rapidly spike blood glucose levels. Cyclical keto is a popular approach that appeals to many, as it's a more flexible way of eating that's easy to maintain long term.

Intuitive keto

An intuitive keto approach embraces keto as more of a lifestyle than a regime. This is the approach that I take. It's very low carb by nature, which allows most people to fluctuate in and out of ketosis, without tracking carbs. It's like cyclical keto, only more intuitive, as the name suggests. The majority of the time you follow a very low-carb diet (20–50 grams of net carbs per day), then when you feel as though you want to eat a sweet potato, you have the freedom to do so because you're not locked into any specific restrictive plan. Just as with cyclical keto, carbs should be sourced from starchy root vegetables (think carrot, beetroot or parsnip). You'll probably evolve from a strict keto diet to a more intuitive approach the more accustomed you become to low-carb foods and a low-carb way of eating.

Targeted keto

A targeted keto approach is different from cyclical keto in that carbs are eaten with specific objectives. This approach, most often adopted by athletes and fitness fans, targets eating carbs around when you exercise, as it is believed to enhance performance. Depending on the type of exercise, the duration of your exercise and the frequency, adding carbs around your workouts can provide immediate fuel if eaten before a workout, or help replenish glycogen stores if eaten afterwards. Anecdotally, women may find that increasing carbs around their menstrual cycle helps keep their cycle regular if a keto diet has caused irregularity.

TESTIMONIAL

I have been a professional strength and conditioning coach in elite sport for 12 years, and in the industry a lot longer. Schooled in the 'high carbohydrate to fuel performance' sports nutrition paradigm, I have watched athletes and myself grow unhealthier by the year. At 40 years of age and after much research before adopting a ketogenic diet, I am far out performing my 18-year-old self. The keto diet has increased my productivity, health, endurance and life performance. Now I want to drive this message and lifestyle home to others.

Chris, 40 years

CUSTOMISING KETO TO WORK FOR YOU

While there are general recommendations that apply across the board for following a keto diet, it can be customised to suit your preferences, lifestyle and individual needs. For example, a keto diet may look very different for someone needing to lose a lot of weight, who lives a sedentary lifestyle and who has some metabolic damage to work through in comparison to someone who is lean, very active and metabolically flexible. Athletes will be able to 'get away' with eating more carbohydrates and protein than someone who is not active. This is simply due to athletic types depleting glucose and glycogen more frequently and encouraging the body to burn fat.

Testing ketones can be useful for customising your keto diet, especially in the early stages while you are working through the kinks. Testing ketones and blood glucose can help you adjust the macronutrients your body needs to achieve ketosis, although this will always remain optional. Possible adjustments you might need to make are increasing fat, experimenting with protein levels to find your upper protein limit and maybe even adding more fibre-rich vegetables. Working with a keto-savvy nutritionist or dietitian is one way to help customise the diet to suit your needs, but you can also experiment for yourself and see what works.

Ultimately, you want to find an approach that is sustainable. If cycling carbs around your workouts enhances your performance, then go with it. If you are someone who does well with restriction and trying to live with moderation almost always fails you, then maybe a rigid keto diet is for you, maybe even consider trying carnivore keto (see page 22 for more).

At the end of the day, there are a number of ways to approach a keto diet, and it's important to remain open and honest with yourself to find what works best for you, your mind, your body and your lifestyle.

~~~~~~~~~~~~~~~~~~~~~~~~~~~~~~~~~~~~~~

TESTIMONIAL

 Two years ago, while working as a carer, I injured my arm, which turned into a frozen shoulder. I was told I could not work if I wasn't 100 per cent well, which was terrible and I worried I wouldn't be able to work again. Not only was I in agony 24/7, I also couldn't move or exercise at all. I did some research and found that the keto diet has an anti-inflammatory effect for conditions like this, so I thought 'why not give it a try?'. Within 2 weeks my weight started dropping and I began to feel good. At Christmas I went overboard and ate way too much non-keto food and, almost immediately, my shoulders were in agony again. This was when I realised just what an effect keto was having on my pain level. After this, I vowed not to over indulge and have since lost 20 kg.

Joanne, 49 years

Vegan keto

Vegan keto can get a bit tricky, but that doesn't mean it's impossible. If you don't consume animal products, don't fret – nature has your back and has supplied many plant-based sources of fat that make it possible to follow a vegan keto diet. Quality sources of plant-based fats come from coconuts (and coconut oil), avocados (and avocado oil), olives (and olive oil), nuts and seeds, including hemp seeds and hemp oil. Protein, however, will come in the form of a powdered supplement, as plant-based proteins in nature are usually packed with carbohydrates. I don't recommend soy products, but if you must include them, go for fermented ones, such as tempeh (sparingly).

Vegetarian or pescetarian keto

Vegetarian keto is one level less restrictive than vegan keto and is actually a very sustainable approach. Foods you can include are eggs, dairy (although I don't encourage it, and if you are going to eat dairy, fermented is best) and if you allow it, seafood too. Eggs and fish are fantastic sources of quality protein and fats.

Full spectrum keto

This almost got the title 'Everything Goes Keto' but that's just not true. There are certainly variations of a keto diet that are less than optimal, ones that include highly-processed vegetable oils, packaged low-carb 'treats' and artificial sweeteners. What we mean by 'full spectrum' is choosing the ratio of plant to animal foods that works best for you, while adhering to a diet based on wholefoods. This means mainly meat, eggs, fish, poultry, low-carb fibre-rich vegetables, nuts and seeds.

Carnivore keto

Most people who adopt this way of eating are on a healing journey or have extreme food sensitivities. Essentially an animal-based diet – where only meat, seafood, eggs and in some cases dairy are eaten – carnivore keto is the newest addition to the keto family or, come to think of it, maybe the oldest. Ketosis appears to be a pleasant side effect of this keto variation, which may require the least strategy of all the versions, as carbs are cut out altogether.

WHO IS THE KETO DIET FOR?

Let me preface this by saying that, at the very least, no-one at any age should be consuming processed carbs such as flours and refined sugars. And let's add refined vegetable oils to that list, too.

When it comes to the keto diet, this way of eating is suitable for a wide range of people. In general, a keto diet is well suited to people leading busy lifestyles, those needing a mental boost, endurance athletes and really anyone interested in optimal health. The keto diet is also suited to those who need to lose weight, are metabolically damaged or insulin resistant. Of course, if you have any health issues (especially problems metabolising fats) and are on medication, going on a keto diet should be done under medical supervision. You must consult your doctor before making any adjustments to your diet and medication.

Keto for women and children

Decades of research, even century-old research, tells us that the ketogenic diet can be safely administered in children and women.[24] Many children, under medical supervision, follow well-formulated keto diets for disease management. These especially modified versions allow for more protein, which helps prevent potential side effects of the diet during developmental years.

Having said that, however, it's generally not recommended that children follow a keto diet if they don't require it, as protein, good fats and quality carbohydrates support optimal growth and development. The most common yet still increasingly rare side effect is stunted growth in children.[25] For this reason, as well as the scientific controversy around the keto diet, I don't recommend children go on a keto diet unless for medical reasons.

Similarly, women are more vulnerable to dietary changes than men, simply due to hormonal differences. The keto diet is very safe for women, but there is no one response all women will experience. It's important you listen to what your body is telling you. Women who are coming to keto overweight, insulin resistant and/or with fertility issues typically respond well to low-carb diets. There is a growing body of evidence to support a keto diet for polycystic ovary syndrome (PCOS), which is tightly linked to insulin resistance.[26]

A common side effect of a keto diet is eating less without realising it. This can be an issue for underweight and/or very active women and can result in irregular menstrual cycles and amenorrhea. If you experience these symptoms, consider how much you are eating and don't be afraid to cycle carbs back into your diet.

Pregnant and breastfeeding women should be cautious about adopting any major dietary changes and I recommend you always consult your healthcare professional before doing so.

THE SYNERGY BETWEEN FASTING AND KETO

When we fast, we derive energy in the same way as when we follow a keto diet – from fat and ketones. Fasting and a keto diet complement each other nicely and are often practised together.

But why would you want to fast in the first place?

In our modern world we live with abundance. Many of us struggle with having too much – too much access to food, too much processed food and, based on statistics, too much body fat. Most of us never give our body an extended period of time without food, and this isn't what we evolved for. The recommendation to eat six small meals a day, with grains and carbs at the base of the food pyramid, may lead to over consumption and weight gain, and doesn't give our body the chance to repair in between meals.

Fasting, on the other hand, swings the pendulum in the opposite direction and restores the natural cycle between the eating and fasting state, allowing the body to repair and recover. It's hard to imagine a time when we didn't live indoors with artificial lights and a fridge full of food. For most of human history eating would have taken place during daylight hours only, or in the case of a failed hunt or no food to gather, eating wouldn't have taken place at all. The adaptations humans made to deal with this are now being explored for their health benefits, and that's why people all around the world are fasting, despite having access to food.

Without constantly having to digest food from the moment we wake up to the moment we go to bed, the body has time to focus on other important tasks, such as cleaning out components of our cells that are no longer serving us and rebuilding new, healthier cells. It turns out, giving our bodies a break from food provides benefits that go beyond weight loss (although responsible fasting can certainly be effective for this). Fasting is now being touted by some health practitioners for its possible health benefits.

There are a number of ways to fast that vary based on length of time and frequency.

Daily intermittent fasting is the most popular approach and involves an eating and a fasting window contained within a 24-hour period.

Most people follow the 16/8 protocol, which means you fast for 16 hours and eat within an 8-hour window. Fasting anywhere from 12 to 16 hours a day should really be the norm. If you are new to fasting, I recommend starting with a 12-hour fast and progressing over a week or two until you close in on 16 hours. You can accomplish this by pushing breakfast out to later in the day, say, to around 11 am, and finishing dinner at around 7 pm; or by eating breakfast earlier in the day and shifting dinner to an earlier time. Ultimately, it comes down to personal preference and what suits your schedule best.

Choosing an eating window that aligns with the sun can help train your circadian rhythms to optimise almost all the body's functions, including metabolism. This is known as time-restricted eating: you consume food within an 8–12-hour period during daylight and fast when the sun has set.

Some people find they do well on just one meal a day and end up fasting for around 22–24 hours. This certainly isn't for everyone, but I have seen people thrive on this way of eating, and so wanted to include it as an option. If daily intermittent fasting isn't for you, maybe experiment with a weekly 24-hour fast, or a monthly 2–3 day fast (after consultation with your health practitioner, of course).

Generally, a fast should include water only; however, black tea or coffee and herbal teas may make it easier, more enjoyable and won't affect your fast too much. For extended fasts, bone broth, although it contains some calories, can be used to help you get through it, while also supplying those all-important electrolytes.

From nutritional ketosis to fasting ketosis and vice versa

Beginning a fast coming off a keto diet, when you are already in a state of nutritional ketosis, can make fasting a whole lot easier, whether that's deliberate or by accident.

Remember that following a keto diet means you have access to fat, that virtually limitless fuel. Because of this you might find you naturally end up fasting without much conscious effort. You get busy, you're caught up at work and by the time you look at the clock it's 3 pm and you realise you haven't eaten all day. If you're confused about how someone would ever forget to eat and need to implement a fasting schedule, that's okay. But don't be surprised when that day comes after you've been following a keto diet for some time. My point is, entering a fast in ketosis, deliberate or not, allows you to skip the uncomfortable transition period you would experience coming from a high-carbohydrate diet. Essentially, a keto diet helps you skip the worst part of fasting – switching from sugar burning to fat burning.

Having said all that, this isn't a one-way street. Fasting enhances your keto diet, too. If you want to ensure you enter ketosis, fasting is the answer. It removes any possible source of glucose, well ... all food for that matter, guaranteeing you produce ketones once the liver has been sufficiently emptied of its glucose stores. However, fasting is obviously not a sustainable long-term approach for achieving ketosis. Depending on your age, your activity level, your metabolic flexibility, among other factors, fasting to enter ketosis will take anywhere from 12–24 hours; 12 really only accounting for the very beginning stages of producing ketones.

So, fasting complements the keto diet by promoting ketosis. After all, the purpose of a keto diet is to achieve ketosis, and fasting certainly helps with this. In fact, if you implement a form of intermittent fasting alongside your keto diet, this may allow you to stay in ketosis and be less stringent with your eating plan – in essence, giving you more wiggle room for protein and low-glycaemic carbs.

It's important to understand that fasting may not be right for you, especially beyond 16–18-hour daily fasts. Make sure you consult your healthcare professional before you start. This is particularly important for anyone on medication that fasting may interfere with, such as medication for type 2 diabetes, hormonal imbalances, kidney disease or cancer. Fasting is also not recommended for anyone under the age of 18, the elderly or pregnant and breastfeeding women.

HOW TO GO KETO

FIVE SIMPLE STEPS TO GO KETO

▶ Step 1: Get rid of refined carbs

Don't worry about the carbs you are eating right now. Rather, focus on removing refined sugars, grains and grain-based foods such as pasta and bread (aka refined carbs) from your diet. Removing processed carbs will turn your focus to wholefoods, which is a great starting point for transitioning to a healthy keto diet. In the meantime, your carbs will come from foods like fruits, vegetables, nuts and seeds.

'It's best to get refined carbs out of the house altogether – out of sight, out of mind!'

▶ Step 2: Embrace healthy fats

I'm going to be honest with you, if you have a fear of fat, a keto diet can be difficult. When you avoid fat while also avoiding carbs, you are left with lean protein and non-starchy vegetables. In this case, there is a lot of room for error, since you are more likely to overeat lean protein and/or carbs to the point that prevents ketone production. Instead, replace the carbs with high-quality healthy fats. For cooking, oils and fats that can handle a little heat with the least risk of oxidation (breakdown of fat into potentially dangerous compounds) are saturated fats like coconut oil, lard and tallow and, if you permit dairy, grass-fed butter and ghee. Use extra-virgin olive oil and avocado oil for cooking at lower temperatures; they are also great in salad dressings or to drizzle over meat, seafood and vegetables.

Wholefood sources of healthy fats can come from grass-fed meats, pastured eggs, wild-caught seafood, avocados, nuts and seeds. Cacao butter (the fat from cacao beans) is also a great source of fat and is delicious in baked goods. Finally, the most keto of them all is MCT oil (see page 259). MCT oil contains a unique type of fat that upon digestion is sent directly to the liver and rapidly converted to ketones, supplying the body with immediate energy. MCT oil is great blended into coffee, smoothies and salad dressings.

▶ Step 3: Eat adequate protein

Fat gets all the attention on a keto diet but protein is, arguably, the key player of any eating plan. Protein provides the building blocks (amino acids) we rely on to repair our bodies, build and maintain muscle and support a healthy immune system. Beyond this, protein does one thing we all appreciate – it keeps us feeling full. Protein is the most satiating macronutrient, meaning it helps us to feel full for longer between meals. The amount of protein you need depends on your body weight, your goals and your activity level, but generally falls within 1.5–1.8 grams per kilogram of body weight (around 25 per cent of your daily energy). Opt for fattier cuts of meat, as they will support your protein requirements and keep you in ketosis.

▶ Step 4: Hydration and electrolytes

When you adopt a low-carb diet, you naturally lose a lot of water, which accounts for the dramatic weight loss many people experience in their first couple of weeks. This loss of water can cause unwanted side effects that can't be solved by simply drinking more water. The issue is due to loss of electrolytes through urine. For every gram of glycogen in the body, there is roughly 3–4 grams of water, so when we burn through our glycogen stores, we lose a lot of water, too. Electrolytes can be lost alongside water and this can cause electrolyte imbalances. The keto diet also keeps insulin levels low, and insulin plays a major role in sodium levels (insulin stimulates sodium reabsorption). If you are not having enough salt with your food, you risk depleting the body of sodium and that may result in potassium wasting. This is what commonly causes the 'keto flu' but can easily be avoided. I recommend making friends with salt to avoid these electrolyte imbalances. If you experience muscle cramping or headaches, supplementing with potassium and magnesium is not a bad idea. You can also use bone broths with some sea salt or Himalayan salt added.

▶ Step 5: Eat wholefoods

When packaged foods are all around you, it's tempting and, I'll admit it, convenient to opt for a bar labelled 'keto' when you don't know what to eat. No measuring, weighing or calculating is involved, the amount of carbs is right there on the nutrition label. There's no label to refer to when you turn over a head of broccoli or an egg, but the awesome thing about choosing low-carb wholefoods is that you don't have to count carbs because your carbs come from non-starchy vegetables that are high in fibre. If you're confused about what to eat, don't worry, by the end of this book you'll have a better understanding of what qualifies as a low-carb option. Just know that if you base your diet on real food, tracking and counting carbs is optional. In the beginning, to get your bearings, it may help to track which foods to eat and which have sneaky carbs, but once you get over the learning curve, it will be smooth sailing ahead. Whole foods will always win over packaged foods and will help make sure you get the proper vitamins and minerals you need.

HOW TO KNOW WHEN YOU ARE IN KETOSIS

The only sure way to know if you are in ketosis is to test for ketones. It can be especially useful in the early stages of a keto diet. Here are the three main methods.

1 ▸ Blood ketones

Testing the blood for ketones is the most accurate way to measure ketosis. You'll need a blood ketone meter and ketone tests strips to check for the ketone BHB. A reading at or above 0.5 mmol/L is indicative of ketosis, and it usually won't exceed 3.0 mmol/L unless you are engaging in a multi-day fast.

2 ▸ Urine ketones

Testing urine is a cost-effective way to test for the ketone AcAc. However, this method does come with a couple of caveats. Ketones are filtered through the kidneys and whatever isn't needed by the body is excreted in urine as waste product. The more keto adapted you are, the fewer ketones you excrete. Testing urine can be a reliable method in the beginning but loses accuracy over time. Keep in mind this method is also influenced by your hydration status. If you are dehydrated, your urine might register higher ketone levels that don't necessarily represent ketosis. Ketone levels are indicated by the colour code found on the packaging. Ketosis is typically defined by urine ketone levels above 15 mg/dL.

3 ▸ Breath ketones

Breath ketone meters are an accurate and easy way to test for the ketone acetone. The upfront cost is generally more, but if you plan on testing frequently, it makes sense in the long term. The concentration of acetone in your breath correlates well with the amount of BHB in your blood, making this a reliable way to measure ketosis. Different meters produce their own unique readings, however ketosis is typically represented with readings above 2 parts per million (ppm) and can reach up to 40 ppm.

TESTIMONIAL

I have had palmar and plantar hyperhidrosis (excessively sweaty hands and feet) since I was a child and over the years it has had a negative effect on my life, leading to anxiety and depression. Just before my 21st birthday, I vowed to do everything in my power to solve this problem, no matter what it took. For the next 10 years I invested untold amounts of time and money seeking the advice of over 25 health professionals, both conventional and alternative. I even consulted with a Buddhist Master direct from Tibet. Not one of these professionals or approaches managed to stop the sweating. None of them considered that the low-fat, high-carb diet I had adhered to my whole life could be the problem. At a live event run by Pete, I was inspired to buy a book called *Primal Body, Primal Mind* by Nora Gedgaudas. Within 48 hours of eating keto my sweating stopped and it hasn't come back.

William, 31 years

Signs that you're in ketosis without testing ketones

IMPROVED FOCUS AND MENTAL CLARITY

If you notice you're less distracted throughout the day and are more productive than you've ever been, it's likely your brain is running on ketones. It's also quite common for people to report feeling a sense of euphoria when in ketosis – heightened awareness and mental clarity. Mental performance is entwined with the amount of energy you have access to and when you're in ketosis, that's essentially infinite. Cutting carbs from your diet and no longer relying on them to feed your brain helps eliminate swings in mental performance.

LONG-LASTING ENERGY

Sugar is quick-burning fuel. It comes in, does its job and whatever isn't used is stored away in the body for later use. However, as I've already mentioned, your body has a limited capacity to store sugar and requires frequent feeding to keep your energy levels stable. In ketosis, when you have full access to your fat stores to make ketones, your energy is sustained throughout the day, no longer fluctuates and is not tied to food and when you eat it.

'FRUITY' BREATH

This may seem like an odd symptom, but when you are in ketosis, you expel ketones when you exhale, due to the breakdown of AcAc to acetone (this is what you test for when using a breath ketone meter). Acetone can have a fruity smell and if noticeable on the breath is a good indicator that you are in ketosis.

DIMINISHED CRAVINGS AND APPETITE CONTROL

In a similar way to how your energy can fluctuate with changes in your blood glucose levels, your appetite can too. Without having access to your fat stores when blood glucose levels fall, you must consume more food, which can trigger cravings for carbs. The keto diet is known for blunting appetite and being incredibly satiating. If you find you are now going for longer periods without having to eat, don't need to snack between meals and intermittently fast with ease, then there's a good chance you have become a fat burner and are in ketosis.

'In ketosis, when you have full access to your fat stores ... your energy is sustained throughout the day, no longer fluctuates and is not tied to food and when you eat it.'

KETO FOOD
PYRAMID

**NUTS, SEEDS AND
LOW-CARB FRUITS**

**BONE BROTH AND FERMENTED
VEGETABLES AND DRINKS**

NIGHTSHADES AND LOW-CARB VEGETABLES

VERY LOW-CARB VEGETABLES

LEAN MEAT AND FISH

HERBS AND SPICES

HEALTHY FATS AND OILS

FATTY FISH AND MEAT, OFFAL AND EGGS

CARBOHYDRATES IN COMMON INGREDIENTS

It can be helpful to measure your net carbohydrate intake when first transitioning to a ketogenic diet. The table on page 34 shows the net carbs found in the ingredients most commonly used when eating keto. These figures are estimations only – the exact amount of carbohydrates found in these ingredients can vary depending on where and how the ingredient is grown, the particular variety of fruit or veg, whether it's in season and also how you cook it.

The difference between net carbs and total carbs

If you do decide to keep track of your carbs when first starting out, make sure you subtract the fibre from the total carb count. Fibre is an indigestible carbohydrate that isn't absorbed into our system and therefore doesn't affect our blood sugar. To work out the net carbs, just subtract the fibre from the total carbs. For example, 100 grams of almonds contains 22 grams of total carbs and 12 grams of fibre, so the net carb count is 10 grams.

Total carb count – fibre count = net carbs

Macros and why macro breakdowns are not featured in this book

You may have heard people discussing macronutrients or 'macros' in relation to keto diets. Macros are the three key nutrients that all foods break down into: fat, protein and carbs. As you'll notice, I don't include the macro breakdown for the recipes in this book. I chose to do this because our bodies are so different in the way they metabolise food and I think it's important to not get too prescriptive over the exact macronutrient percentages. It is generally more useful to look at your approximate macro breakdown for the whole day rather than obsessing over the macros of each individual meal.

In my intuitive approach to the keto diet (see page 19), I always try to listen to my body and take notice of how I feel after eating particular ingredients or meals. Tuning into your body – perhaps even keeping a journal of how you feel each day or after each meal – really is the best way to figure out if the amount of carbohydrates, proteins and fats is right for your body. And as I always say, as long as you are basing your meals around nutrient-dense wholefoods, you will be on the right track.

Ingredient	Net carbohydrates
Almonds (28 g)	3
Apple (100 g)	11
Artichoke (globe) (100 g)	3
Avocado (100 g)	2
Banana (100 g)	20
Blackberries (100 g)	5
Blueberries (100 g)	12
Bok choy (100 g)	1
Brazil nuts (28 g)	1
Broccoli (100 g)	4
Brussels sprouts (100 g)	5
Cabbage (100 g)	4
Capsicum (100 g)	4
Carrot (100 g)	7
Cashews (28 g)	8
Cauliflower (100 g)	3
Celery (100 g)	2
Chia seeds (28 g)	2
Clams (100 g)	4
Coconut flour (28 g)	6
Coconut water (250 ml)	7
Cucumber (100 g)	3
Dates (100 g)	71
Eggs (1 large)	<1
Fennel (100 g)	4
Fish (100 g)	0
Flaxseeds (28 g)	1
Kale (100 g)	6
Kombucha (250 ml)	7

Ingredient	Net carbohydrates
Lettuce (100 g)	<3
Liver (chicken) (100 g)	1
Macadamia nuts (28 g)	2
Meat (chicken, beef, pork) (100 g)	0
Mussels (100 g)	7
Okra (100 g)	4
Olives (28 g)	1
Onion (100 g)	8
Orange (100 g)	9
Oysters (100 g)	5
Parsnip (100 g)	13
Pecans (28 g)	1
Pistachios (28 g)	4
Pumpkin (100 g)	6
Pumpkin seeds (28 g)	3
Radish (100 g)	2
Raspberries (100 g)	6
Rocket (100 g)	2
Sesame seeds (28 g)	0
Silverbeet (100 g)	3
Spinach (100 g)	1
Strawberries (100 g)	5
Sunflower seeds (28 g)	4
Sweet potato (100 g)	17
Tomato (100 g)	3
Unsweetened cacao (28 g)	6
Walnuts (28 g)	1
Zucchini (100 g)	2

KETO KITCHEN ESSENTIALS

Filling your pantry, fridge and freezer with the right ingredients is the key to successfully embracing the keto approach to eating. If you only have nutrient-dense wholefoods on hand, it is so much easier to stay on track and not be tempted by highly processed or higher carb foods. Here is my go-to guide to get you started.

Pantry

Apple cider vinegar (raw)

Cacao butter

Cacao powder (raw and unsweetened)

Coconut flour

Coconut milk/cream

Coconut, shredded

Collagen powder* (grass fed and marine)

Dried herbs

Fire tonic (medicinally spiced apple cider vinegar drink)

Fish, jarred* (such as preserved anchovies, salmon, tuna, mackerel and sardines)

Fish sauce (sugar free)

Gelatine powder* (grass fed)

Lemons and limes

Nut and seed flours (such as almond meal)

Nuts (almonds, cashews, macadamias, pecans, walnuts)

Oils (coconut, extra-virgin olive, avocado, MCT)

Salt* (unrefined varieties, such as sea, Himalayan)

Seaweed (dulse,* nori,* wakame)

Seed crackers

Seeds (hemp, chia, pumpkin, sunflower, sesame)

Spices (turmeric, black pepper, paprika, cumin)

Sprout seeds (broccoli, radish)

Supplements (iodine, magnesium)

Sweeteners* (liquid stevia, monk fruit, xylitol, erythritol, honey)

Tahini

Tamari or coconut aminos*

Tomatoes, jarred (see Note page 86)

Vanilla (pods, powder or paste)

See Glossary for more information on these ingredients

Fridge

Bacon, ham and salami (free range and nitrate free)

Coconut yoghurt

Curry pastes

Dressings (homemade)

Eggs (organic and free range)

Fermented drinks (dairy-free kefir, kombucha) (see page 217)

Fermented vegetables (kimchi, sauerkraut) (see pages 252 and 257)

Fish and shellfish

Ghee* (if choosing to include dairy)

Good-quality animal fat* (lard, tallow, duck fat)

Herbs (basil, parsley, mint, coriander)

Kelp noodles and other sea vegetables

Keto bread (see page 251)

Low-carb fruits (blueberries, raspberries, blackberries, strawberries)

Low-carb vegetables (cucumbers, celery, lettuce, tomatoes, silverbeet, cabbage, spring onions, radishes, cauliflower, broccoli)

Mayonnaise

Meats (all varieties, fattier cuts)

Nut and seed butters

Nut cheeses

Nut milks (coconut, cashew, almond) and hemp milk

Offal

Olives

Pâté

Pickles

Salmon roe/caviar

Sprouts

Sriracha chilli sauce (see page 256)

Tomato ketchup (see page 257)

Freezer

Avocados (diced, for adding to smoothies and treats)

Bananas (chopped, for adding to smoothies on high-carb days)

Berries (blueberries, raspberries, blackberries, strawberries)

Bone broth (beef, chicken, pork) (see pages 245, 246 and 253)

Bones for making broth

Keto bread (see page 251), sliced

Leftovers (to ensure you always have something healthy on hand when you need to eat)

Lemon and lime juice (frozen in ice-cube trays)

YOUR GO-TO FATS AT A GLANCE

Embracing a range of healthy fats is the cornerstone of the keto diet, as they provide us with energy, keep us feeling full for longer, provide us with a range of vitamins and help support our nervous and digestive systems. Here are my favourite fats and oils – keep your kitchen stocked with these to nourish your body and ensure that your food is always full of flavour.

For cooking

- Animal fats, such as rendered chicken and duck fat, lard and tallow
- Coconut oil
- Ghee (if choosing to include dairy)

For dressings and drizzling over finished dishes

- Avocado oil
- Extra-virgin olive oil

For adding to smoothies and treats

- Hemp oil
- MCT oil

QUICK AND EASY SNACKS

Once you have gone into ketosis and start burning fat for fuel, you'll find that you no longer need to snack between meals like you used to, as your body has large stores of fat to use for energy. However, when you are first starting out, it might be useful to have some easy and healthy snack options to help keep you on the right track. You can even make these up in advance and keep them in the pantry or fridge so that they are ready to go whenever you need.

- Hard-boiled eggs with a dollop of Japanese mayo (see page 251)
- Avocado slices sprinkled with furikake (see page 248) and wrapped in nori sheets
- Handful of nuts or seeds
- Cup of bone or vegetable broth (see pages 76, 78 and 79)
- Celery or cucumber sticks dipped in nut butter or tahini
- Chocolate and coconut gummies (see page 240)
- Kale chips
- Small bowl of kimchi (see page 252) or turmeric kraut (see page 257)
- Keto bread (see page 251) with avocado smash (see page 52)

BREAK

FAST

GREEN KETO BOWL

Avocado in a smoothie has to be one of life's great pleasures. When avocados are plentiful and at their peak, I like to buy a lot and scoop out and freeze the flesh, so I always have some on hand for super creamy and healthy smoothies. I've also included MCT oil for another great dose of fat.

50 g (1 cup) baby spinach leaves

1 handful of mint leaves, plus extra to serve

1 avocado, halved and flesh scooped out

125 ml (½ cup) coconut cream or plant-based milk

½–1 tablespoon MCT oil* or coconut oil

½–1 tablespoon collagen* powder

35 g (¼ cup) ice cubes

sweetener of your choice (liquid stevia,* xylitol,* monk fruit sweetener,* honey), to taste (see Note)

1 teaspoon hemp seeds*

1–2 tablespoons mixed seeds (pumpkin, sunflower and flaxseeds, activated if possible*)

* See Glossary

Place the spinach, mint, avocado, coconut cream or milk, MCT oil or coconut oil, collagen and ice cubes in a high-speed blender and whiz until smooth. Add the sweetener to taste.

Pour the smoothie into a bowl and top with the hemp seeds, mixed seeds and extra mint leaves.

NOTE If using xylitol or monk fruit sweetener, blend it in a high-speed blender or spice grinder until it is the texture of icing sugar before adding it to the smoothie – this will help it to dissolve easily in the cold mixture.

CHIA AND BLUEBERRY SMOOTHIE BOWL

SERVES 2

Chia seed smoothie bowls are an excellent breakfast to make up ahead of time. Sometimes on a Sunday, I make these and keep them in the fridge, so the kids have them ready to go for the next day or two. You can top yours with whatever you like, such as low-carb fruit or cacao nibs, activated nuts or seeds or even, as I've done here, some paleo muesli.

400 ml coconut cream or plant-based milk, plus extra if needed
150 g coconut yoghurt
sweetener of your choice (liquid stevia,* xylitol,* monk fruit sweetener,* honey), to taste (see Note opposite)
½ teaspoon vanilla powder or paste
80 g chia seeds
1 small handful of blueberries
8 blackberries
100 g Paleo Muesli (page 253) (optional)
1 tablespoon flaxseeds
edible flowers, to serve (optional)

* See Glossary

Place the coconut cream or milk, yoghurt, sweetener and vanilla in a blender and whiz until smooth. Add the chia seeds and blend for a few seconds until combined with no lumps. If needed, add a little more coconut cream or milk and blend.

Pour the mixture into two serving bowls and sprinkle on the berries, muesli (if using) and flaxseeds. Decorate with edible flowers if desired.

HEMP SEED PORRIDGE WITH BLUEBERRY COMPOTE

SERVES 2

Hemp seeds are the perfect keto choice for porridge, as they are roughly 70 per cent fat, 25 per cent protein and 5 per cent carbs. When teamed with your choice of milk – such as coconut, nut or hemp – and the addition of low-carb fruits like berries, you create a keto breakfast that is a fun way to get healthy plant-based fats into your diet. Always try to source wild, organic blueberries if possible.

150 g hemp seeds*

500 ml (2 cups) coconut or plant-based milk of your choice, plus extra to serve

2 tablespoons shredded coconut

2 tablespoons ground flaxseeds

1 tablespoon chia seeds

1 teaspoon manuka honey or sweetener of your choice (liquid stevia,* xylitol,* monk fruit sweetener*), to taste

a pinch of sea salt

¼ teaspoon vanilla powder or paste

BLUEBERRY COMPOTE

200 g blueberries

1 tablespoon manuka honey or sweetener of your choice (liquid stevia,* xylitol,* monk fruit sweetener*), to taste

* See Glossary

To make the blueberry compote, place half the blueberries and the honey or sweetener in a small saucepan over low heat. Cook for 5 minutes until the blueberries have slightly broken down. Remove from the heat, stir through the remaining berries and allow to cool.

Combine the hemp seeds, milk of your choice, coconut, flaxseeds, chia seeds, honey or sweetener and salt in a small saucepan over medium–low heat. Cook, stirring frequently, for 5–7 minutes, or until thickened. Stir in the vanilla.

Transfer the porridge to serving bowls, pour over some extra milk, then spoon over the blueberry compote and serve.

SCRAMBLED EGGS WITH SALMON AND KIMCHI

I have heard from some of you that my recipes have too many ingredients, and I hear what you say, but sometimes, to take a dish to the next level, you need to ramp up the flavour – and that means adding more. For example, here I've added furikake seasoning, a Japanese seaweed and spice mix. It takes about 5 minutes to make and once that's done, you have it on hand to use for months. The same rule applies to the kimchi. When you have spice blends and fermented foods in your pantry and fridge, adding depth and flavour to very simple meals becomes super easy.

4 eggs

3 tablespoons melted coconut oil or good-quality animal fat*

sea salt and freshly ground black pepper

4 slices of smoked trout or salmon

½ Lebanese cucumber, finely sliced

60 g Kimchi (page 252)

½ teaspoon finely snipped chives

1 teaspoon Furikake Seasoning (page 248)

extra-virgin olive oil, for drizzling

* See Glossary

Crack the eggs into a large bowl, add 2 tablespoons of the melted coconut oil or fat and whisk to combine. Season well with salt and pepper.

Heat the remaining oil or fat in a non-stick frying pan over medium heat. Pour in the egg mixture and cook for 1 minute, lifting and pushing the mixture from the outside of the pan to the centre with a wooden spoon. Remove from the heat and gently fold the mixture a few times. Allow the eggs to stand for 30–60 seconds so that the residual heat finishes the cooking.

Divide the scrambled eggs between serving plates, add the smoked trout or salmon, cucumber and kimchi. Sprinkle the chives and furikake seasoning over the scrambled eggs, then drizzle on some olive oil and serve.

CAULIFLOWER-CRUSTED QUICHE BITES

MAKES 9

People love quiches – they are quick and delicious, and you can whip up a heap of them to have on hand for whenever you are hungry. Plus, they make for a wicked school or work lunch. Here, to make them anti-inflammatory and keto, I replace the traditional shortcrust pastry with a cauliflower crust. Have a play with different fillings: smoked trout or salmon, prawns, salami and mushrooms all work well.

360 g (2 cups) cooked Cauliflower Rice (page 246), chilled
1 tablespoon coconut oil or good-quality animal fat*
1 egg
sea salt and freshly ground black pepper

FILLING
3 eggs
1 tablespoon melted coconut oil or good-quality animal fat*
2 rindless bacon rashers, finely chopped
½ long red chilli, deseeded and sliced (optional)
1 handful of baby spinach leaves, chopped

* See Glossary

Preheat the oven to 180°C (160°C fan-forced).

Lightly grease nine holes of a standard muffin tray and line with baking paper.

Place the cauliflower rice in a clean tea towel, bring the edges together and twist to squeeze out the excess water. Tip the cauliflower rice into a bowl, add the coconut oil or fat and egg, season to taste and mix well.

Press the cauliflower crust mixture into the base and side of each prepared muffin hole. Bake for 15 minutes, or until slightly golden around the edge.

Meanwhile, to make the filling, crack the eggs into a bowl, add the coconut oil or fat, bacon and chilli (if using) and lightly beat to combine. Season with salt and pepper.

Spoon the filling evenly into each cauliflower crust, then top with the spinach.

Reduce the oven temperature to 160°C (140°C fan-forced), return the muffin tray to the oven and bake for 10–15 minutes until the filling is golden and set.

CHILLI CRAB SCRAMBLE

SERVES 4

Chilli crab was one of the first ever dishes I cooked on television over 20 years ago. To this day people come up to me to say it is still a favourite they love to cook at home. Recently, I came across the most amazing crabmeat from Fraser Island in Queensland and, taking inspiration from my chilli crab recipe, reimagined it into something super quick and delicious. This scramble is a modern version of chilli crab for people on the go. You can replace the crabmeat with prawns, bacon, sausages, or lamb or beef mince. I like to serve turmeric kraut (page 257) with this dish.

8 eggs

2 teaspoons fish sauce

2 tablespoons coconut oil or good-quality animal fat*

200 g cooked crabmeat (spanner, Alaskan king or blue swimmer)

2 tablespoons Sriracha Chilli Sauce (page 256)

2 radishes, finely sliced

1 small handful of alfalfa sprouts

Turmeric Kraut (page 257), to serve

SALAD

1 handful of mixed salad leaves

1 handful of coriander leaves

2 spring onions, green part only, sliced diagonally

1 red Asian shallot, finely sliced

2 tablespoons lime juice

80 ml (⅓ cup) olive oil

1 handful of mung bean sprouts

sea salt and freshly ground black pepper

* See Glossary

Crack the eggs into a bowl, add the fish sauce and whisk to combine.

Heat the coconut oil or fat in a non-stick frying pan over medium heat. Pour in the egg mixture and stir gently for 3 minutes, lifting and pushing the mixture from the outside of the pan to the centre with a wooden spoon. Add the crabmeat and continue to stir until the eggs are almost set (about 15 seconds). Remove from the heat and gently fold the mixture a few times. Allow the eggs to stand for 30–60 seconds so that the residual heat finishes the cooking.

Combine all the salad ingredients in a bowl and gently toss. Taste and season with more salt and pepper if needed.

Divide the scramble among bowls and drizzle over the sriracha. Arrange the salad, radish, alfalfa and kraut on the side and serve.

AVOCADO SMASH ON TOAST WITH SMOKED SALMON

SERVES 4

It may seem a little clichéd to include avo on toast here, but I am a sucker for it and love to make it for the whole family. What we put with ours changes all the time; sometimes it's crispy bacon, at other times poached eggs or cooked prawns, and one of our favourites is smoked salmon and roe with sprouts, cress or herbs. It's always good to give your avo a generous hit of lemon juice to cut through the richness. If you don't have time to make keto bread, feel free to roast field mushrooms instead or cook eggs just the way you like them to go with the avo smash.

8 slices of Keto Bread (page 251), toasted

12 slices of smoked salmon

2 tablespoons salted baby capers, rinsed and patted dry

1 small handful of alfalfa sprouts

1 small handful of baby kale sprouts or sprouts of your choice

3 tablespoons salmon roe

extra-virgin olive oil, for drizzling

½ red onion, very finely sliced (optional)

1 lemon, cut into wedges

AVOCADO SMASH

2 avocados, roughly chopped

1 teaspoon lemon juice, or to taste

1 tablespoon extra-virgin olive oil

sea salt and freshly ground black pepper

* See Glossary

Place all the avocado smash ingredients in a bowl and roughly mash with a fork. Taste and season with a little more salt and pepper if needed.

Spread the avocado smash over the toast, then top with the smoked salmon. Sprinkle on the capers, alfalfa and kale sprouts, then spoon over the salmon roe. Drizzle over some olive oil and finish with a sprinkle of salt and pepper. Serve with the red onion (if using) and lemon wedges on the side.

BACON AND EGG BOWL

If you are looking for ways to invigorate your bacon and egg breakfast, I encourage you to give this flavoursome bowl a try. Soft-boiled or hard-boiled eggs, depending on how you fancy yours, are combined with smooth avocado, crispy bacon, crunchy lettuce, toasted keto bread croutons and, to tie everything together, a delicious dressing.

8 rindless streaky bacon rashers

4 slices of Keto Bread (page 251)

3 tablespoons extra-virgin olive oil

8 eggs

4 baby cos lettuces, leaves separated and torn

2 avocados, cut into wedges

1 large handful of flat-leaf parsley leaves

1 small handful of micro herbs (optional)

8 jarred salted anchovy fillets, rinsed and patted
   dry, finely chopped

TARRAGON AND ANCHOVY DRESSING

2 egg yolks

4 jarred salted anchovy fillets, rinsed and patted
   dry, chopped

1 garlic clove, crushed

1 tablespoon lemon juice, plus extra if needed

1 teaspoon Dijon mustard

250 ml (1 cup) extra-virgin olive oil

sea salt and freshly ground black pepper

1 teaspoon finely chopped tarragon

Preheat the oven to 180°C (160°C fan-forced). Lightly grease a baking tray.

Arrange the bacon in a single layer on the prepared tray and bake for 15–18 minutes until golden brown and crisp. Set aside.

Meanwhile, to make the tarragon and anchovy dressing, combine the egg yolks, anchovy, garlic, lemon juice and mustard in a food processor. Process briefly until combined. With the motor running, slowly pour in the olive oil in a thin steady stream until the dressing has emulsified and thickened slightly. Add the oil a little faster until you have added it all, then add 2 teaspoons of water and process until the dressing is the consistency of pouring cream. Taste and add salt and pepper or more lemon juice if desired. Pour into a bowl and mix through the tarragon. Set aside until needed.

Place the bread on another baking tray, brush both sides with the olive oil and season with salt. Set the oven to grill and toast the bread until golden on both sides. Cut into bite-sized pieces and set aside.

Bring a saucepan of water to the boil over high heat. Reduce the heat to medium, add the eggs and simmer for 6 minutes for soft-boiled, or cook to your liking. Drain and, when cool enough to handle, peel the eggs under cold running water, cut in half lengthways and set aside.

Divide the cos leaves, avocado and bacon among serving bowls. Add the soft-boiled eggs, then scatter over the parsley, micro herbs (if using), anchovy and keto bread. Drizzle over the dressing, season with salt and pepper and serve.

ITALIAN SAUSAGES AND EGGS

I must tell you a secret: I wasn't a fan of sausages until I was an adult. Now that's out, I can reveal that for the last three decades or so, sausages have become one of my favourite things to eat and I search them out all over the world. Hands down, blood sausages are my favourite of all. Here is one of the healthiest meals I cook every week and each time I choose a different type of sausage. I like to cook up a heap, so I have leftovers in the fridge to sneak as a cold snack.

3 tablespoons coconut oil or good-quality animal fat*

8 Italian pork and fennel sausages or sausages of your choice

4 eggs

HERB SAUCE

1 handful of flat-leaf parsley leaves

1 tablespoon tarragon leaves, chopped

1 jarred salted anchovy fillet, rinsed and patted dry, chopped

1 garlic clove, finely chopped

1 tablespoon lemon juice

150 ml olive oil

sea salt and freshly ground black pepper

* See Glossary

To make the herb sauce, place the parsley, tarragon, anchovy, garlic and lemon juice in a food processor and process until the herbs are finely chopped. With the motor running, gradually drizzle in the olive oil and blitz until combined. Season with salt and pepper to taste.

Heat 2 tablespoons of the coconut oil or fat in a large frying pan over medium heat. Add the sausages and cook for 8 minutes, or until browned and just cooked through. Remove the sausages from the pan and set aside, keeping warm.

Meanwhile, heat the remaining oil or fat in a non-stick frying pan over medium heat. Crack in the eggs and cook for 2–3 minutes or until cooked to your liking. Season with salt and pepper and slide the eggs onto serving plates. Place the sausages next to the eggs, spoon over the sauce and serve.

BONE MARROW ON TOAST

I love the way everything old becomes new again. This dish of roasted bone marrow on toast is traditional country fare. Even if you are not a fan of bone marrow, I urge you to try it like this, just once, because everyone I have ever made it for has absolutely enjoyed it. I use keto bread here; for a classic combination, replace the bread with a minute steak.

2 beef marrow bones, cut crossways into 5 cm rounds (ask your butcher)
sea salt and freshly ground black pepper
6 slices of Keto Bread (page 251)
extra-virgin olive oil, for brushing

PARSLEY SALAD
2 tablespoons red wine vinegar or apple cider vinegar
1 ½ tablespoons salted baby capers, rinsed and patted dry
1 red Asian shallot, finely sliced
2 large handfuls of flat-leaf parsley leaves
2 Garlic Confit cloves (page 250), finely chopped (optional)
2 tablespoons extra-virgin olive oil

Preheat the oven to 220°C (200°C fan-forced).

Place the marrow bones on a baking tray and season with salt and pepper. Roast in the oven for 15–20 minutes until cooked through and golden.

To make the parsley salad, combine the vinegar, capers and shallot in a bowl and season with a pinch of salt. Allow to stand for 5 minutes to pickle the shallot. Next, add the parsley, garlic confit (if using) and olive oil and gently toss.

Meanwhile, heat a chargrill pan over medium–high heat. Lightly brush the bread with olive oil and cook in batches for 1–2 minutes on each side until charred. Set aside, keeping warm.

When ready to serve, place the marrow bones and warm toast on serving plates and add the salad.

WELL
BOW

NESS
LS

'PAD THAI' WITH CRISPY SALMON

Crispy-skinned salmon never gets old or boring, especially when you team it with an amazing dressing and some fresh ingredients to balance out the rich and nutritious fat in the fish. I'm a huge advocate of wild-caught salmon from New Zealand or overseas – unfortunately, in Australia all our salmon is farmed. If you can't find wild salmon, I suggest you look for other wild fish or seafood, such as kingfish, barramundi, sardines or prawns as a substitute.

2 tablespoons coconut oil or good-quality animal fat*
4 x 170 g salmon fillets, skin on, pin-boned
1 large carrot, cut into matchsticks
1 large zucchini, cut into matchsticks
1 red capsicum, deseeded and cut into matchsticks
150 g snow peas, cut into matchsticks
250 g red cabbage, finely shredded
1 small beetroot, cut into matchsticks
1 long red chilli, deseeded and finely sliced
2 spring onions, green part only, finely sliced diagonally
1 handful of bean sprouts, rinsed and drained well
3 tablespoons Crispy Shallots (page 247)
1 small handful of mint leaves
1 small handful of Thai basil leaves
1 handful of coriander leaves
80 g (½ cup) cashew nuts, toasted and chopped

ALMOND AND DRESSING
3 tablespoons almond butter
3 tablespoons lime juice
2 ½ tablespoons tamari or coconut aminos*
1 teaspoon fish sauce, plus extra if needed
3 teaspoons honey (optional)
1 teaspoon toasted sesame oil
1 ½ teaspoons finely grated ginger
3 kaffir lime leaves, finely chopped
1 garlic clove, crushed
1 bird's eye chilli, deseeded (leave the seeds in if you like it hot) (optional)
sea salt

* See Glossary

To make the almond and lime dressing, place all the ingredients in a high-speed blender, add 3 tablespoons of water and whiz until smooth. Taste and add a little extra salt or fish sauce if needed.

Preheat the oven to 200°C (180°C fan-forced).

Heat the coconut oil or fat in a large, non-stick, ovenproof frying pan over medium–high heat. Season the salmon on both sides with salt. Add the salmon, skin-side down, to the pan and cook for 1 minute. Transfer the pan to the oven and roast the salmon for 3–4 minutes until the skin is golden and crisp. Remove the pan from the oven, flip the salmon over and set aside to cook for 30 seconds, or until medium–rare. (The residual heat will continue to cook the salmon, so the pan doesn't need to be placed over heat.) Rest the salmon for 2 minutes before serving.

To serve, arrange the carrot, zucchini, capsicum, snow pea, cabbage, beetroot, chilli, spring onion and bean sprouts in four serving bowls. Cut the salmon into bite-sized pieces and add to the salad. Spoon the dressing over the top and finish with the crispy shallots, herbs and cashews.

SMOKED TROUT AND BROCCOLI BOWL

Smoked fish has become one of my staple foods as it has a long shelf life, is packed full of satiating healthy fats and proteins, and the smoky component is next-level yum. In this recipe I add broccoli, a nutritional powerhouse that goes well with smoked fish. Include some kraut, avocado and seeds and we are done and dusted in the most delicious and nourishing way. To mix things up, swap out the smoked fish for fresh fish or roast chicken.

1 large head of broccoli (about 400 g), broken into small florets

70 g kale leaves (about ¼ bunch), stems discarded and leaves torn

300 g savoy cabbage, finely shaved

1 whole hot-smoked rainbow trout (about 400 g), skin and bones removed and flesh flaked

2 spring onions, green part only, cut into matchsticks

1 handful of mint leaves

1 handful of flat-leaf parsley leaves

1 handful of dill sprigs

1 large handful of Spiced Seeds (page 256)

2 tablespoons salmon roe

LEMON DRESSING

80 ml (⅓ cup) extra-virgin olive oil

juice of 1 lemon, or to taste

1 tablespoon apple cider vinegar

sea salt and freshly ground black pepper

AVOCADO PUREE

1½ avocados, roughly chopped

80 g coconut yoghurt or Mayonnaise (page 252)

2 tablespoons extra-virgin olive oil

1 tablespoon lemon juice

1 garlic clove, finely chopped

Bring a saucepan of salted water to the boil. Add the broccoli and blanch for 4 minutes, or until the broccoli is cooked but slightly crunchy in the middle. Drain and plunge the broccoli into ice-cold water to stop the cooking process. Drain again and set aside.

Place all the lemon dressing ingredients in a bowl and whisk well.

Combine the kale and cabbage in a bowl, pour on half the lemon dressing and season with salt and pepper. Massage the dressing into the vegetables with your hands. Set aside.

Next, place the avocado puree ingredients in a food processor and blitz until smooth. Season with salt and pepper.

Arrange the kale mixture, broccoli and smoked trout in serving bowls, spoon on the avocado puree and scatter the spring onion, herbs, spiced seeds and salmon roe over the top. Drizzle on the remaining lemon dressing if desired. Any leftover dressing can be stored in the fridge for up to 5 days.

SPICY AHI POKE

The classic poke (pronounced po-kay) bowl of diced raw fish is one of the main dishes of native Hawaiian cuisine. Ahi is the name tuna is given in Hawaii and some parts of the USA; here in Australia we call it yellowfin. Tuna is pretty mild in flavour and can really use a boost, which is why you often see it spiced with red chilli, wasabi or a combination of both. I love to mix the raw fish with toasted sesame seeds, creamy avocado and a spicy sauce.

360 g (2 cups) cooked Cauliflower Rice
    (page 246), chilled
2 avocados, diced
2 large handfuls of watercress

SPICY TUNA
400 g sashimi-grade tuna, cut into 1.5 cm cubes
2 tablespoons tamari or coconut aminos*
2 teaspoons toasted sesame oil
1 spring onion, finely chopped
1 tablespoon yuzu juice*
2 tablespoons olive oil
2 teaspoons finely grated ginger
2–3 teaspoons Sriracha Chilli Sauce (page 256),
    or to taste

YUZU MAYONNAISE
100 g Japanese Mayonnaise (page 251)
2 teaspoons yuzu juice* or lemon juice
¼ teaspoon ground turmeric
sea salt and freshly ground black pepper

TO SERVE
sesame seeds, toasted
dulse flakes*

* See Glossary

Combine all the spicy tuna ingredients in a bowl and gently toss. Cover and place in the fridge to marinate for 5 minutes.

Meanwhile, place all the yuzu mayonnaise ingredients in a small bowl and mix well. Taste and season with more salt and pepper if needed.

Divide the cauliflower rice among four serving bowls, top with the spicy tuna, avocado and watercress, then add a spoonful of yuzu mayonnaise. Finish with a sprinkle of sesame seeds and some dulse flakes.

NASI GORENG WITH SARDINES

In Australia and New Zealand sardines are often not revered for their taste or nutritional profile. In my opinion, they outclass pretty much every other fin fish except for perhaps wild-caught salmon. They are abundant, rich and full flavoured with a high oil content and you can eat them nose to tail – yep, head and all! That makes them a valuable and sustainable food source. Here I have teamed them with a paleo–keto version of nasi goreng, that classic Indonesian fried rice dish with loads of flavour. Delicious!

80 g duck fat or good-quality animal fat*

3 spring onions, white and green parts separated, finely sliced

1 carrot, finely chopped

½ celery stalk, finely chopped

4 garlic cloves, finely chopped

2 teaspoons shrimp paste

2 bird's eye chillies, deseeded and finely chopped (leave the seeds in if you like it hot), plus extra to serve if desired

2 tablespoons chopped coriander leaves, plus extra leaves to serve

720 g (4 cups) uncooked Cauliflower Rice (page 246)

1½ tablespoons tamari or coconut aminos*

2 teaspoons honey (optional)

2 eggs

sea salt and freshly ground black pepper

10 sardine fillets, skin on

1 handful of bean sprouts, rinsed and drained

2 tablespoons Crispy Shallots (page 247) (optional)

lime cheeks, to serve

* See Glossary

Heat 2 tablespoons of the fat in a wok or large frying pan over medium heat. Add the white part of the spring onion, the carrot and celery and stir-fry for 5 minutes, or until slightly softened. Stir in the garlic, shrimp paste, chilli and coriander and fry for 1 minute, or until fragrant. Add the cauliflower rice, tamari or coconut aminos and honey (if using) and continue to stir-fry for about 5 minutes, or until everything is combined and the cauliflower is cooked through.

Next, heat 1 tablespoon of fat in a non-stick frying pan over medium heat. Crack in the eggs and cook for 2–2 ½ minutes until the egg whites have set, or cook to your liking. Season with some salt and pepper.

Meanwhile, heat the remaining fat in a large, heavy-based frying pan over high heat. Season the sardine fillets with salt and pepper, then add them to the pan, skin-side down and in batches if necessary, and cook for 15 seconds. Flip and cook for a further 5 seconds, then remove from the pan.

Divide the fried cauliflower rice among serving bowls, top each with the sardines and an egg, then scatter over the green part of the spring onion, the bean sprouts, coriander leaves and, if you like, some crispy shallots and extra chilli. Serve with lime cheeks on the side for squeezing over.

JERK CHICKEN SALAD BOWL

Jerk chicken or jerk anything (pork, lamb, goat, beef, seafood) has got to be one of the best recipes in the world as this tasty marinade elevates the flavour of even the humblest ingredients. Here I've paired jerk chicken with roast pumpkin, pomegranate seeds, green goddess dressing and some fresh leaves to create a delicious and abundant salad bowl.

4 chicken thigh cutlets, bone in, skin on
80 ml (⅓ cup) melted coconut oil or good-quality animal fat*
1 bunch of kale (about 300 g), stems discarded and leaves chopped
1 tablespoon extra-virgin olive oil
2 tablespoons lemon juice
600 g kent pumpkin, cut into large chunks
1 large red onion, cut into wedges
200 ml Green Goddess Dressing (page 250)
1 handful of baby sorrel leaves or mixed baby salad leaves
seeds of ½ pomegranate

JERK MARINADE
1 red onion, chopped
6 large garlic cloves, crushed
4 scotch bonnet or habanero chillies, deseeded and chopped
3 tablespoons tamari or coconut aminos*
3 tablespoons white wine vinegar or apple cider vinegar
1 tablespoon honey (optional)
2 teaspoons thyme leaves
1 tablespoon sweet paprika
2 teaspoons ground allspice
1 teaspoon freshly ground black pepper
1½ teaspoons sea salt
½ teaspoon ground cinnamon
¼ teaspoon freshly grated nutmeg

* See Glossary

Combine all the jerk marinade ingredients in a food processor and blitz to form a smooth paste.

Transfer the marinade to a large shallow bowl, add the chicken and turn to coat. Cover and refrigerate for at least 1 hour or overnight for best results.

Preheat the oven to 180°C (160°C fan-forced).

Heat 2 tablespoons of the coconut oil or fat in a large frying pan over medium–high heat. Add the chicken in batches and seal for 5 minutes on all sides until browned. Transfer the chicken to a roasting tin and roast for 35–40 minutes, basting with the marinade occasionally, until the chicken is golden and cooked through. Transfer to a plate and rest for 5 minutes, keeping warm.

Meanwhile, place the kale in a large bowl and pour over the olive oil. Rub the oil into the kale with your hands for a couple of minutes. (This removes the waxy coating from the kale and allows it to absorb the dressing.) Pour over the lemon juice, toss and set aside for at least 30 minutes to soften.

Place the pumpkin and onion in a roasting tin, toss with the remaining coconut oil or fat and season with salt and pepper. Roast for 20–25 minutes until golden and cooked through.

Arrange the kale in serving bowls, top with the roast pumpkin and onion, then add the chicken. Spoon on the green goddess dressing and finish with the sorrel or salad leaves and pomegranate seeds.

CHICKEN BIBIMBAP

In Korean bibim means 'mixing various ingredients' and bap means 'rice'. As this is a paleo-inspired ketogenic book, I have swapped out the rice for low-carb cauliflower rice, while keeping the traditional integrity of the dish by using high-quality ingredients that are full of flavour.

2 tablespoons coconut oil or good-quality animal fat*
600 g boneless chicken thighs, cut into 1.5 cm strips
3 garlic cloves, finely chopped
½ teaspoon finely ground black pepper
2 tablespoons tamari or coconut aminos*
2 teaspoons honey (optional)
2 tablespoons shaoxing wine or dry sherry
1 teaspoon apple cider vinegar

SEASONED BEAN SPROUTS
½ teaspoon sea salt
200 g bean sprouts, rinsed and drained
1 tablespoon toasted sesame oil

SEASONED CARROT
2 teaspoons coconut oil
2 carrots, cut into 5 cm batons
½ teaspoon sea salt

SPICY CUCUMBER
2 Lebanese cucumbers, sliced
1 teaspoon sea salt
1–2 teaspoons Fermented Chilli Sambal (page 248) or finely chopped red chilli, plus extra to serve
2 teaspoons sesame seeds, toasted

SEASONED SPINACH
300 g English spinach leaves, trimmed
2 teaspoons toasted sesame oil
1 teaspoon sea salt

TO SERVE
360 g (2 cups) cooked Cauliflower Rice (page 246)
200 g Turmeric Kraut (page 257) or Kimchi (page 252)
4 egg yolks
1 spring onion, finely sliced

* See Glossary

Heat 1 tablespoon of the coconut oil or fat in a wok or large, heavy-based saucepan over high heat. Add the chicken in batches and fry for 1–2 minutes until sealed. Remove the chicken from the pan and set aside.

Reduce the heat to medium, add the remaining oil or fat and the garlic and pepper and stir-fry for 10 seconds, or until fragrant. Pour in the tamari or coconut aminos, honey (if using), shaoxing or sherry and vinegar and bring to the boil. Return the chicken to the pan and stir-fry for 4–5 minutes until the chicken is cooked through.

To make the seasoned bean sprouts, place the salt, bean sprouts and 125 ml of water in a saucepan and bring to the boil. Reduce the heat to low, cover and simmer for 1 minute. Drain and transfer the sprouts to a bowl. Mix in the sesame oil and set aside.

To make the seasoned carrot, melt the coconut oil in a frying pan over medium heat. Add the carrot and salt and stir-fry for 2 minutes, or until just tender. Set aside.

To make the spicy cucumber, toss the cucumber and salt in a large bowl and set aside for 5 minutes. Gently squeeze the cucumber with your hands to remove any excess liquid. Transfer to a clean bowl and stir in the fermented chilli sambal or red chilli and sesame seeds, then set aside.

To make the seasoned spinach, fill a large saucepan with water and bring to the boil. Add the spinach and cook for 1 minute. Drain and rinse under cold water. Then, taking a handful of spinach at a time, gently squeeze out the water. Place the spinach on a chopping board and chop into 5 cm pieces. Transfer to a bowl, add the sesame oil and salt and mix well.

Divide the cauliflower rice among serving bowls, top with the seasoned veggies, turmeric kraut or kimchi, chicken and an egg yolk. Sprinkle over the spring onion and serve with some extra sambal or chilli on the side. The egg yolk will cook when tossed through the warm dish.

SEARED BEEF POKE

This simple recipe ticks the boxes for flavour and nutrition and is one your whole family will love to tuck into. It's also very quick to prepare, which makes it perfect for weeknights. Beautifully seared steak is finely sliced and teamed with an assortment of herbs and salad ingredients, then a delicious dressing and mayo complete the dish.

3 garlic cloves, finely grated

1 tablespoon finely grated ginger

1½ tablespoons tamari or coconut aminos*

1 tablespoon toasted sesame oil

1 tablespoon honey (optional)

1 tablespoon apple cider vinegar

600 g beef eye fillet, halved crossways

1 tablespoon coconut oil or good-quality
   animal fat*

1 teaspoon black and white sesame seeds, toasted

½ sheet of nori, finely sliced

1 handful of micro herbs (optional)

Japanese Mayonnaise (page 251), to serve

DRESSING

2 tablespoons tamari or coconut aminos*

2 teaspoons toasted sesame oil

2 tablespoons yuzu juice* or lemon juice

SALAD

½ red onion, finely sliced

250 g cherry tomatoes, cut into quarters

1–2 Lebanese cucumbers, chopped

2 spring onions, cut into matchsticks

2 radishes, sliced

1 handful of coriander leaves

1 large handful of baby mesclun leaves

1 large handful of snow pea sprouts

* See Glossary

Place the garlic, ginger, tamari or coconut aminos, sesame oil, honey (if using) and vinegar in a large bowl and mix to combine. Add the beef and turn to coat. Cover and set aside to marinate at room temperature for 1 hour.

Heat the coconut oil or fat in a large, heavy-based frying pan over medium heat. When the pan is smoking hot, add the beef and seal for 1 minute on all sides for rare, or cook to your liking. Remove the beef from the pan and rest for 5 minutes, keeping warm, before finely slicing.

Place all the dressing ingredients in a bowl and mix to combine.

Divide the salad ingredients among four serving bowls, top with the beef and drizzle over the dressing. To finish, sprinkle on the sesame seeds, nori and micro herbs (if using) and serve with some Japanese mayonnaise on the side.

SOUPS AND BROTHS

VEGETABLE TEA

I understand that people sometimes want something super light if they are going through emotional turmoil or a challenging time with their health. This nourishing soup of well-cooked vegetables is perfect when you're not feeling your best. You can, of course, add some chicken or fish or use chicken or fish bone broth as the base, if you desire.

1 tablespoon coconut oil or good-quality
  animal fat*
1–2 pinches of sea salt
pinch of ground turmeric (optional)

VEGETABLE STOCK
1 tablespoon coconut oil
1 onion, roughly chopped
2 large carrots, roughly chopped
2 parsnips, roughly chopped
1 celery stalk, roughly chopped
¼ head of cauliflower, broken into florets
4 silverbeet leaves, chopped into 2.5 cm pieces
100 g mushrooms of your choice (field, portobello,
  Swiss brown, button, cup, shiitake), sliced
1 small zucchini, roughly chopped
1 small handful of thyme sprigs
1 small handful of flat-leaf parsley stalks
1 dried bay leaf

* See Glossary

To make the vegetable stock, melt the coconut oil in a stockpot over medium–high heat. Add the onion and sauté for 5 minutes, or until softened. Add the carrot, parsnip, celery and cauliflower and cook for 10 minutes, or until slightly tender.

Add the silverbeet to the pot, pour in 4 litres of water and add the mushroom, zucchini, thyme, parsley and bay leaf. Bring to the boil, then reduce the heat to low, cover and simmer for 3–4 hours until the stock is highly flavoured.

Remove the stock from the heat and strain through a fine sieve, pressing on the vegetables to extract all their juices. Discard the vegetables (unless you are keeping them to use in soups).

To serve, heat 375 ml of the vegetable stock in a saucepan until just simmering. Stir through the coconut oil or fat and season with salt to taste and turmeric (if using). Pour the vegetable tea into a mug and enjoy. Store the remaining vegetable stock in airtight containers in the fridge for up to 4 days or freeze for up to 3 months.

PETE'S SUPER BROTH

Is it bird?

Is it a plane?

No! It's Pete's Super Broth!

Sorry, I couldn't resist. So many foods and diets have been touted as SUPER over the years but in my experience a simple anti-inflammatory diet (no grains, no dairy, no toxic oils, lower carb) seems to be the one that, time and time again, produces sustainable long-term health. Here is a delicious broth I believe has some super goodness to it, including turmeric, ginger, black pepper and lemon juice.

375 ml (1 ½ cups) Chicken Bone Broth (page 246)

½ teaspoon finely grated ginger

½ teaspoon finely grated fresh turmeric or ¼ teaspoon ground turmeric

¼ teaspoon finely grated garlic

½–1 teaspoon lemon juice, or to taste

1 tablespoon coconut oil or good-quality animal fat*

a pinch each of sea salt and freshly ground black pepper

* See Glossary

Heat the broth in a small saucepan until just simmering. Stir in the ginger, turmeric, garlic, lemon juice, coconut oil or fat and salt and pepper.

Pour the broth into a mug and enjoy.

IMMUNE-STRENGTHENING CHICKEN BROTH

I'd like to replace the old saying 'an apple a day keeps the doctor away' with 'some broth a day keeps the doctor away', especially if you include immune-boosting ingredients such as ginger, cayenne pepper, lemon juice and parsley. You can mix this up with a different combination of ingredients – try adding some slippery elm, licorice root and pau d'arco, for gut support. You could also throw in sliced medicinal mushrooms or truffle, bean sprouts and herbs. Other ingredients you might like to include are collagen, gelatine and MCT oil, as well as turmeric, garlic and ashwagandha.

700 ml Chicken Bone Broth
(page 246)
1 tablespoon finely grated ginger
pinch of cayenne pepper
2 teaspoons lemon juice, or to taste
sea salt and freshly ground black
pepper
1 tablespoon finely chopped flat-leaf
parsley leaves

Pour the broth into a saucepan and bring to a simmer over medium heat. Add the ginger, cayenne pepper and lemon juice and stir to combine. Season with salt and pepper.

Pour the hot broth into two glasses or mugs and sprinkle over the chopped parsley. Take a sip and enjoy.

SEAWEED SOUP WITH SALMON AND AVOCADO

For this book, I wanted to offer something quick, easy and a little more satiating than the traditional miso soup. So I have deconstructed the classic salmon and avocado nori roll and reimagined it as a keto-friendly soup, minus the rice. To make it even more substantial, you can add some cauliflower rice and a poached egg. Or if you are avoiding all soy products, simply omit the miso from the broth. And before you ask if avocado works in a soup . . . the answer is a resounding 'Yes!'.

20 g dried wakame*

400 g sashimi-grade salmon, skin off, cut into 5 mm thick slices

2 avocados, sliced

1 teaspoon shichimi togarashi,* or to taste (optional)

BROTH

2 x 10 cm sheets dried kombu*

1.5 litres water, fish broth or Chicken Bone Broth (page 246)

2 teaspoons dashi powder*

100 g white (shiro) miso paste*

* See Glossary

You'll need to start this recipe a day ahead.

To start on the broth, place the kombu and water or broth in a large, heavy-based saucepan. Set aside to allow the kombu to soak for at least 8 hours or overnight.

The next day, place the pan over medium–high heat and bring to a simmer (do not boil). Reduce the heat to low and simmer for 15 minutes. Add the dashi and continue to simmer for 5 minutes, then remove from the heat and allow to steep for 15 minutes. Strain and discard the kombu.

Soak the wakame in 250 ml of water for 5 minutes, or until the wakame expands, then drain.

Whisk the miso into the broth and bring back to a simmer. Add the wakame and simmer for 2 minutes, or until it is heated through.

Ladle the broth into soup bowls. Add the raw salmon and avocado, sprinkle on the shichimi togarashi (if using) and serve.

SPICED CHICKEN SOUP WITH OKRA

SERVES 4

I love the unique taste and texture of okra and always buy some when I visit the Asian grocer. If you have never tried it, adding a few pods to a soup or curry is a great way to experience this wonderful ingredient. You will notice that okra, when cut and cooked, has a somewhat slimy texture, but that is what makes it so special. Once you learn to appreciate the slime factor, a whole new world awaits you in the kitchen. Feel free to include some chilli or cayenne pepper in your broth if you like a little heat.

3 tablespoons coconut oil or good-quality animal fat*

2 onions, chopped

20 fresh curry leaves

4 garlic cloves, chopped

1 tablespoon finely grated ginger

2 teaspoons ground turmeric

2 teaspoons ground cumin

½ teaspoon ground cinnamon

1.5 litres Chicken Bone Broth (page 246)

1 large sweet potato (about 350 g), cut into 2 cm cubes

10 fresh okra pods, cut into 2 cm pieces

400 ml coconut milk

sea salt and freshly ground black pepper

2 ½ teaspoons lemon juice, or to taste

4 boneless chicken thighs, skin on

1 large handful of baby spinach leaves

* See Glossary

Heat 1 tablespoon of the coconut oil or fat in a large saucepan over medium heat. Add the onion and curry leaves and sauté for 5 minutes, or until softened. Add the garlic, ginger and spices and cook for 1 minute, or until fragrant.

Pour in the broth, add the sweet potato and bring to the boil. Reduce the heat to low and simmer for 20 minutes, or until the flavours develop and the sweet potato is almost tender. Add the okra and cook for a further 8 minutes, or until the okra and sweet potato are tender.

Stir the coconut milk into the broth, bring to a gentle simmer and season with salt and pepper. Remove from the heat and stir in the lemon juice.

Meanwhile, preheat the oven to 200°C (180°C fan-forced).

Brush the chicken with the remaining oil or fat and season generously with salt and pepper.

Heat a large ovenproof frying pan over medium–high heat. Add the chicken, skin-side down, and cook for 3 minutes, or until golden. Flip and cook for a further 1 minute, or until sealed and lightly golden. Transfer the pan to the oven and roast for 8 minutes, or until the chicken is cooked through. Place on a plate and rest for 5 minutes, keeping warm, before thickly slicing.

Place the chicken in serving bowls and add the baby spinach. Ladle over the broth and finish with a good grind of pepper.

CHINESE MEATBALL SOUP

One of the things I love about the way soups and broths are made in Asia is the dedication to ensuring they are healthy and so damn tasty you keep coming back for more. Here is a super simple meatball soup made with minimal fuss and packed full of flavour and nutritional goodness. Your whole family will love it.

1.5 litres Chicken Bone Broth (page 246)

3 tablespoons tamari or coconut aminos*

3.5 cm piece of ginger, cut into matchsticks

2 garlic cloves, finely sliced

150 g shiitake mushrooms (or your favourite variety of mushroom), sliced

1 spring onion, green and white parts separated and finely sliced

2 baby bok choy, trimmed

MEATBALLS

250 g raw prawn meat (see Note)

500 g pork mince

2 teaspoons toasted sesame oil

2 tablespoons gluten-free oyster sauce

2 garlic cloves, finely grated

1 spring onion, finely chopped

2 tablespoons shaoxing wine or dry sherry

½ teaspoon fine sea salt

½ teaspoon freshly ground black pepper

* See Glossary

To make the meatballs, place the prawn meat in a food processor and pulse a few times until finely chopped. Place the prawn mince, pork mince and the remaining meatball ingredients in a bowl and mix well. Cover and refrigerate for at least 30 minutes.

With clean wet hands, roll the mixture into walnut-sized balls. Set aside.

Pour the broth into a large saucepan, add the tamari or coconut aminos, ginger and garlic and bring to a simmer over medium heat. Add the mushroom and white part of the spring onion and continue to simmer for 15 minutes to develop the flavour.

Add the bok choy to the soup, then carefully drop in the meatballs. Cook for 6–7 minutes until the meatballs are cooked through.

Ladle the soup into warm bowls, sprinkle over the green part of the spring onion and serve.

NOTE If you'd prefer to make these without the prawn meat, you can simply replace it with the same amount of extra pork mince.

ITALIAN LAMB SHANK SOUP

When preparing meals for others, it goes without saying that we want to make our food as yummy as possible. Yes, yummy is the word I like to use, as it helps me take my chef apron off and instead put on my home-cook apron. It makes me think about my family and friends and whether they'll love it, rather than focus on the bells and whistles of a restaurant dish. And this soup ticks all the home-cooking boxes: it is nourishing, moreish and extremely yummy without having to overthink anything.

3 lamb shanks (each about 450 g)
sea salt and freshly ground black pepper
2 tablespoons coconut oil or good-quality animal fat*
2 large onions, finely chopped
2 celery stalks, chopped
4 large garlic cloves, finely chopped
1 tablespoon chopped oregano leaves
600 g whole peeled tomatoes, crushed (see Note)
1.9 litres Chicken Bone Broth (page 246) or water
2 fresh bay leaves
400 g kent pumpkin, peeled and cut into 2.5 cm cubes
2 zucchini, halved lengthways and sliced
2 silverbeet leaves, stems and leaves separated and chopped
finely grated zest and juice of ½ lemon
2 tablespoons chopped flat-leaf parsley leaves

* See Glossary

Season the lamb shanks well with salt and pepper.

Heat the coconut oil or fat in a large, heavy-based saucepan over medium–high heat, add the lamb shanks and sear for 4 minutes on all sides until well browned. Transfer the shanks to a plate and set aside.

Reduce the heat to medium, add the onion and celery to the pan and sauté for 5 minutes, or until softened. Stir in the garlic and oregano and sauté for 1–2 minutes. Add the tomatoes and cook, stirring occasionally, for 3–4 minutes. Pour in the broth or water and add the bay leaves, then return the shanks to the pan and bring to the boil. Reduce the heat to low, cover with a lid and simmer for 1½ hours.

Add the pumpkin, zucchini and silverbeet stems to the soup and season with salt and pepper. Simmer for a further 40 minutes, or until the meat is falling off the bone. Remove the lamb shanks and, when cool enough to handle, remove the meat from the bone and shred or chop.

Meanwhile, add the silverbeet leaves to the soup and cook for 5 minutes, or until wilted. Return the meat to the pan and stir well. Taste and adjust the seasoning and squeeze in the lemon juice.

Ladle the soup into warm bowls, sprinkle on the parsley and lemon zest and serve.

NOTE I prefer to buy diced and whole peeled tomatoes in jars rather than cans, due to the presence of Bisphenol A (BPA) in some cans. BPA is a toxic chemical that can interfere with our hormonal system.

MEXICAN BEEF AND VEGETABLE SOUP

When I'm creating recipes for my cookbooks, the first thing I ask myself is: will people make this at home? There's no point in putting a recipe in a book if it's too daunting. The second question is: how can I make the healthiest and tastiest version of this recipe? I want every dish to make my family and all who eat it smile. The third question is: how can I simplify it without losing flavour? And, with these three questions in mind, my amazing team and I come up with a collection of recipes that we turn into a healthy cookbook. I can promise you that this Mexican-inspired soup has passed this test with flying colours – it is incredibly simple and delicious, and I hope it brings a smile to the face of everyone you cook it for.

2 tablespoons coconut oil or good-quality animal fat*

700 g blade steak (or another cut of beef that is good for stewing), cut into 2.5 cm cubes

2 onions, chopped

4 garlic cloves, finely chopped

1 long red chilli, deseeded and chopped (optional)

2 carrots, cut into 2 cm cubes

2 teaspoons Mexican spice blend

1 teaspoon ground cumin

400 g whole peeled tomatoes, crushed (see Note page 86)

1.25 litres Beef or Chicken Bone Broth (page 245 or 246)

2 zucchini (about 250 g), halved lengthways and sliced

2 yellow squash, chopped

250 g broccoli, broken into small florets

sea salt and freshly ground black pepper

coriander leaves, to serve

* See Glossary

Heat 1 tablespoon of the coconut oil or fat in a large, heavy-based saucepan over medium–high heat. Add the beef in batches and cook for 3 minutes on all sides until browned. Transfer to a plate and set aside.

Reduce the heat to medium, add the remaining oil or fat and the onion to the pan and sauté for 5 minutes, or until softened. Stir in the garlic and chilli (if using) and sauté for 30 seconds, or until fragrant. Add the carrot, spice blend, cumin, tomatoes and broth, then return the beef to the pan and stir. Bring to the boil, then reduce the heat to low, cover with a lid and simmer for 1½ hours.

Add the zucchini, squash and broccoli to the soup and simmer, uncovered, for a further 30 minutes, or until the beef is very tender. Season with salt and pepper.

Ladle the soup into warm bowls, top generously with coriander leaves and serve.

LIGHT MEALS AND EN

TREES

COCONUT-CRUMBED PRAWNS WITH SWEET CHILLI SAUCE

This dish takes me back to my early days as an apprentice chef living on the Gold Coast and working in a seafood restaurant. We used to have to crumb tubs and tubs of prawns and calamari and, to be honest with you, after an hour or so it wasn't that much fun, but it used to take a good couple of hours each day to get through it. I actually think it put me off crumbing anything for years after that! Well, I am back and I've gotta say, I do love to crumb many things these days. Nothing can beat wonderfully golden crumbed seafood with a little kick from a delicious sauce.

100 ml coconut milk

4 eggs

150 g tapioca flour*

sea salt and freshly ground black pepper

250 g shredded coconut

20 raw king prawns, shelled and deveined, tails left intact

coconut oil or good-quality animal fat,* for deep-frying

Mayonnaise (page 252), to serve

SWEET CHILLI SAUCE (OPTIONAL)

125 ml (½ cup) lime juice

115 g honey

2 tablespoons fish sauce

4 garlic cloves, peeled

4 cm piece of ginger, finely chopped

3 long red chillies, chopped

* See Glossary

If you are making the sweet chilli sauce, place all the ingredients in a food processor, add 125 ml of water and process to a paste. Pour into a saucepan and bring to the boil over medium heat. Reduce the heat to low and simmer for 5 minutes, or until the sauce has reduced by half. Remove from the heat and set aside to cool.

Meanwhile, prepare your crumbing station for the coconut prawns. Place the coconut milk and eggs in a shallow bowl and whisk until smooth. Place the tapioca flour in another shallow bowl, season with salt and pepper and mix well. Place the shredded coconut in a third bowl.

Dust the prawns in the seasoned tapioca flour, dip in the egg mixture, then evenly coat in the shredded coconut.

Heat enough coconut oil or fat to reach 3 cm up the side of a large frying pan and bring to about 160°C over medium heat. Add the prawns in batches and fry for 1–1½ minutes until golden and cooked through. Drain on paper towel and allow to rest for 2 minutes. Season with a little salt.

Arrange the prawns on a large platter and serve with the sweet chilli sauce (if using) and mayonnaise for dipping.

NOTE The sweet chilli sauce is completely optional. Feel free to just add some chilli flakes or powder to the mayo instead.

WILD FISH WITH HEMP SEED PESTO

If you start with a beautiful piece of wild fish, you really don't need to do too much to create a delicious meal. Here, I have combined a dairy-free pesto with some hemp seeds for extra goodness to make the fish shine. Some zucchini noodles or roasted mushrooms would make a welcome addition, but there is nothing wrong with keeping things super simple either.

4 x 180 g wild-caught white fish fillets (such as bream, mulloway, whiting, snapper or barramundi), skin on, pin-boned
2 tablespoons coconut oil or good-quality animal fat*

HEMP SEED PESTO
100 g (about ¾ cup) hemp seeds*
1 garlic clove, chopped
50 g (1 cup) baby spinach or rocket leaves (or a mix of both)
1 large handful of basil leaves
finely grated zest and juice of 1 lemon
125 ml (½ cup) extra-virgin olive oil
2 tablespoons nutritional yeast*
sea salt and freshly ground black pepper

TO SERVE
extra-virgin olive oil
hemp seeds*
lemon wedges

* See Glossary

Place all the hemp seed pesto ingredients in a food processor and process to a paste.

Season the fish fillets with salt and pepper.

Heat the coconut oil or fat in a large, heavy-based frying pan over high heat. Add the fish, skin-side down, in batches if necessary, and fry for 2 ½–3 minutes until crispy. Flip over and cook for 2 minutes, or until the fish is just cooked through. Place the fish on a plate and rest for 2 minutes, keeping warm.

Spoon the hemp seed pesto into shallow serving bowls and add the fish. Finish with a drizzle of olive oil and a sprinkle of hemp seeds. Serve with the lemon wedges.

SALMON WITH RADICCHIO SALAD

People have been combining bitter or acidic flavours with fatty seafood or meat for a very long time. Think of terrines and pâtés, which are often teamed with pickles; roast pork with sauerkraut; or Korean barbecue with kimchi. Here I combine some fatty wild salmon with bitter radicchio and a lovely acidic dressing to balance it all to perfection.

2 x 230 g salmon cutlets, halved and centre
    bone removed
2 tablespoons coconut oil or good-quality
    animal fat*
sea salt and freshly ground black pepper
Aioli (page 245), to serve

DRESSING
125 ml (½ cup) extra-virgin olive oil
3 tablespoons red wine vinegar
2 teaspoons Dijon mustard

SALAD
½ head of radicchio, leaves separated and torn
1 large handful of flat-leaf parsley leaves
1 large handful of chervil leaves
1 large handful of mint leaves
100 g Pickled Red Onion (page 253)
2 tablespoons pine nuts (activated if possible),*
    toasted

* See Glossary

Brush the salmon with the coconut oil or fat, then season with salt and pepper. Heat a large, non-stick frying pan over medium–high heat, add the salmon and cook for 2 minutes on each side until the flesh is tender and opaque, or cook to your liking. Place on a plate and rest for 2 minutes, keeping warm.

Place the dressing ingredients in a bowl and whisk well. Season with salt and pepper.

Arrange the salad ingredients on serving plates and pour over the dressing. Add the salmon and a dollop of aioli and serve.

SALMON TATAKI WITH DAIKON AND SPRING ONION PONZU

There is something so satisfying about combining slices of raw wild salmon with a zingy dressing – pop it in your mouth and savour the richness of one of nature's most perfect superfoods. Here is a wonderful example of letting the produce shine without interfering too much – just a little dressing to round it out for taste as well as visual appeal. You can do the same thing with an eye fillet or sirloin steak and it will work equally well.

4 x 120 g sashimi-grade salmon fillets, pin-boned
1 teaspoon melted coconut oil or good-quality
   animal fat*
sea salt and freshly ground black pepper
a pinch of shichimi togarashi*
80 g daikon, finely grated

TAKAKI DRESSING
2 ½ tablespoons tamari or coconut aminos*
125 ml (½ cup) apple cider vinegar
2 tablespoons bonito flakes*

SPRING ONION PONZU
1 tablespoon yuzu juice* or lemon juice
2 spring onions, green part only, finely chopped
3 tablespoons olive oil
1 tablespoon apple cider vinegar
1 teaspoon tamari or coconut aminos*
½ teaspoon finely grated ginger
1 tablespoon grated fresh wasabi or ½ teaspoon
   wasabi paste

* See Glossary

Combine all the tataki dressing ingredients in a bowl then set aside for 20 minutes to allow the flavours to develop. Strain through a fine sieve into a bowl, squeezing the bonito to extract as much liquid as possible; discard the bonito. Set aside.

Place all the spring onion ponzu ingredients in a bowl and mix to combine. Set aside.

Heat a non-stick, heavy-based frying pan over high heat. Lightly brush the salmon with the coconut oil or fat and season with salt and pepper. Sear the salmon for 2–3 seconds on all sides to seal, or cook to your liking.

Place the salmon in the freezer for 10 minutes to firm the outside. (This makes slicing it easier.)

Finely slice the salmon and arrange on a serving plate. Drizzle on the tataki dressing, spoon over the spring onion ponzu and sprinkle on the shichimi togarashi. Place the daikon on the side and serve.

CRACKLING CHICKEN WITH CARROT AND QUANDONG SALAD

I love that native Australia foods, such as the quandong, are becoming more well known. The quandong, or wild peach, has been eaten across the desert regions of Australia for many thousands of years. The fruit is small, shiny and a bright pink–red colour, and is rich in vitamin C and E as well as zinc. With its sweet and sour flavour, quandong is a beautiful addition to any salad. You can buy dried quandong from specialty food stores, some health food stores or online. If you can't find any, you can use unsweetened dried cranberries instead.

6 boneless chicken thighs, skin on
1 tablespoon sea salt
2 teaspoons coconut oil or good-quality animal fat*
1 teaspoon sumac*

SALAD
80 ml (⅓ cup) extra-virgin olive oil
1 tablespoon lemon juice
1 tablespoon apple cider vinegar
1 tablespoon honey (optional)
1 teaspoon grated ginger
1 long red chilli, deseeded and finely chopped (optional)
4 large carrots, grated
1 handful of macadamia nuts (activated if possible),* toasted and chopped
1 large handful of coriander leaves, roughly chopped
1 handful of mint leaves, roughly chopped
1 handful of quandongs
freshly ground black pepper

* See Glossary

Flatten the chicken thighs with a mallet to ensure they cook evenly. Season the skin and flesh with the salt.

Heat the coconut oil or fat in a large, heavy-based frying pan over medium–high heat. Place three of the chicken thighs, skin-side down, in the hot pan. Fry the chicken, undisturbed, for 6–8 minutes until crispy and golden brown. Flip the chicken over and cook for 3 minutes, or until cooked through. Remove from the pan and keep warm. Repeat with the remaining chicken thighs. Allow to rest for 5 minutes, then slice into thick pieces.

Meanwhile, to make the salad, place the olive oil, lemon juice, vinegar, honey (if using) and ginger in a large bowl and whisk until combined. Add the chilli (if using), carrot, macadamia, coriander, mint and quandongs, toss and season well with salt and pepper.

Arrange the salad in a serving dish. Top with the chicken, sprinkle over the sumac and serve.

DUCK LIVER WITH CAPERS AND PINE NUTS

I am a huge fan of offal. Liver seems to be what most people will have a crack at cooking and eating, which is why I love to include liver recipes in my books. I really want to normalise these highly nutritious foods and encourage people to eat them. Here is a quick and delicious duck liver dish with capers, pine nuts, parsley and dried fruit. If you are following a strict keto diet, simply remove or reduce the amount of dried fruit.

700 g duck livers

3 tablespoons coconut oil or good-quality animal fat*

sea salt and freshly ground black pepper

3 garlic cloves, finely chopped

2 tablespoons salted baby capers, rinsed and patted dry

2 ½ tablespoons pine nuts (activated, if possible),* toasted

2 tablespoons raisins or dried wild blueberries

2 large handfuls of flat-leaf parsley leaves

2 tablespoons sherry vinegar

3 tablespoons extra-virgin olive oil

* See Glossary

Rinse the duck livers under cold water, pat dry with paper towel and trim off any fat, sinew and veins. Set aside.

Melt the coconut oil or fat in a large, heavy-based frying pan over medium–high heat. Add the livers and cook for 30–60 seconds on each side until browned and just cooked through (they should still be slightly pink on the inside). Season with a little salt and pepper.

Add the garlic to the pan and cook for 10 seconds, or until fragrant. Stir in the capers, pine nuts, raisins or dried blueberries, parsley, vinegar and olive oil and toss with the livers until warmed through. Serve immediately.

SPICED KANGAROO SALAD

Kangaroo is an often overlooked and misunderstood protein. I am here to encourage people to have an open mind about eating this wonderful native animal. Some people say that the more wild the food is, the more energy it can give us, which is why wild-caught seafood and wild game are promoted in a paleo approach. In this recipe I have added some beautiful native spices to complement the roo and created a delicious salad that will surely make you feel great.

400 g (about 6) baby beetroot
80 ml (⅓ cup) melted coconut oil or good-quality animal fat*
sea salt and freshly ground black pepper
600 g kent pumpkin, peeled and cut into large chunks
4 x 160 g kangaroo loin fillets
80 g sauerkraut
60 g macadamia nuts (activated if possible),* toasted and chopped
40 g (about ⅓ cup) mixed seeds (pumpkin, sunflower and hemp seeds, activated if possible)*

SPICE MIX
1 teaspoon sea salt
1 teaspoon mountain pepper (see Notes)
1 teaspoon ground cumin

SALAD
2 handfuls of salad leaves
100 g samphire (see Notes)
100 g ice plant (see Notes)
3 tablespoons extra-virgin olive oil
2 tablespoons sherry vinegar

HORSERADISH MAYONNAISE
1 tablespoon finely grated fresh horseradish
150 g Mayonnaise (page 252)

* See Glossary

Preheat the oven to 200°C (180°C fan-forced).

Place each beetroot bulb on a piece of foil large enough to enclose. Drizzle over a little of the coconut oil or fat and season with salt and pepper. Wrap up and roast for 30–40 minutes, or until a small knife slides easily through to the centre. Set aside until cool enough to handle. Peel and halve each beetroot, then cut into 1 cm thick wedges.

Meanwhile, rub 2 tablespoons of the oil or fat over the pumpkin, season with salt and pepper and place on a baking tray. Roast for 35–40 minutes until the pumpkin is tender and golden.

Combine the spice mix ingredients in a bowl. Rub the remaining oil or fat over the kangaroo, then sprinkle on the spice mix.

Heat a barbecue grill plate to hot or a chargrill pan over high heat. Add the kangaroo fillets and cook for 5–6 minutes, turning, until charred and cooked to medium–rare. Place the fillets on a plate and rest for 5 minutes, then thickly slice.

To make the salad, place the salad leaves, samphire and ice plant in a bowl. Pour over the olive oil and vinegar and gently mix to coat the leaves. Season with salt and pepper if needed.

Combine the horseradish mayonnaise ingredients in a small bowl.

Divide the salad among bowls. Add the sauerkraut, pumpkin and beetroot and top with the kangaroo. Sprinkle on the macadamia and mixed seeds, add some horseradish mayo and serve.

NOTES Mountain pepper is an evergreen shrub that is grown in cool-temperature rainforests in south eastern Australia. You can find it in specialty food stores, delis or online.

Samphire is a native succulent plant with a crunchy texture and salty burst of flavour. Ice plant is also a native succulent plant. The leaves are juicy with a slightly salty flavour. Both are available from select greengrocers.

ROAST BONE MARROW WITH SALSA VERDE

SERVES 4

Please give this simple entree a try next time you see bone marrow at the butcher. I love to scoop out the marrow and serve it alongside a nice juicy steak. Or, for another layer of moreishness, try it smeared on keto toast and topped with eggs. Experiment and have fun with bone marrow; it works well with meat, seafood, vegetables and egg dishes and is sensational in soups, too.

4 x 12 cm pieces of beef bone marrow, halved
    lengthways (ask your butcher)
sea salt and freshly ground black pepper

SALSA VERDE
300 ml extra-virgin olive oil
2 handfuls of basil leaves
2 handfuls of mint leaves
2 handfuls of flat-leaf parsley leaves
2 garlic cloves, chopped
4 jarred salted anchovy fillets, rinsed and
    patted dry
50 g salted baby capers, rinsed well and patted dry
2 tablespoons lemon juice
50 g (⅓ cup) pine nuts (activated if possible),*
    toasted

Preheat the oven to 200°C (180°C fan-forced).

Season the bone marrow with salt and pepper, place on a baking tray and roast for 15 minutes, or until golden brown.

Meanwhile, combine all the salsa verde ingredients in a food processor and blitz to form a thick paste. Season to taste with salt and pepper.

Place the bone marrow on plates, spoon over the salsa verde and serve immediately.

NOTE Place any leftover salsa verde in a sterilised glass jar, cover with a thin layer of oil, then seal with the lid. Store in the fridge for up to 5 days.

JAPANESE BEEF TATAKI

The word 'tataki' literally means 'pounded', but it does not refer to the preparation of the meat or fish. Instead, it refers to the ginger condiment, which was originally pulverised with a mortar and pestle. However, the term tataki is generally used to refer to seared and very finely sliced meat or fish, which is then marinated or has a vinegar dressing poured over it. It is one of my favourite Japanese meals and is a wonderful way to eat steak or fatty fish like salmon or kingfish in the summer months. It generally doesn't come with too many other items, except for the dressing and maybe some spring onions, however I like to add some more veggies to turn it into a light meal.

coconut oil or good-quality animal fat,* for brushing

600 g beef sirloin, trimmed of fat and halved lengthways (you can also use eye fillet, rib eye or tri-tip)

sea salt and freshly ground black pepper

2 Lebanese cucumbers, spiralised

2 carrots, spiralised

2 teaspoons toasted sesame oil

1 teaspoon sesame seeds, toasted, plus extra to serve

2 spring onions, green parts only, cut into matchsticks

ONION PONZU

1 teaspoon finely grated ginger

1 garlic clove, finely grated

½ onion, finely chopped

3 tablespoons tamari or coconut aminos*

80 ml (⅓ cup) apple cider vinegar

2 tablespoons olive oil

* See Glossary

Place the onion ponzu ingredients in a bowl and mix well. Set aside to steep for at least 20 minutes to allow the flavours to develop.

Heat a barbecue hotplate to hot or place a large, heavy-based frying pan over high heat and brush with some coconut oil or fat. Lightly brush the beef with some oil or fat and season with salt and pepper. Add the beef and sear for 1–1 ½ minutes on all sides to seal, or cook to your liking. Place the beef on a plate and rest for 4 minutes, keeping warm.

Meanwhile, place the spiralised veggies in a bowl, add the sesame oil and sesame seeds and gently toss. Season to taste with salt.

Using a sharp knife, finely slice the beef and arrange on a platter with the spiralised veggies. Drizzle over the onion ponzu, top with the spring onion, sprinkle on some extra sesame seeds and serve.

CURRY AND

SPICE

MOJO PRAWNS

In my opinion this dish should be on the cover of the book, as I prefer my food to be the star – and, I gotta say, grilled prawn heads look a lot better than my mug. Here, I've kept the recipe as simple as possible by grilling whole prawns, heads and all, as is the tradition in many cultures around the world. There is just so much flavour in prawn heads . . . go on, I dare you to give them a try! I've added a mojo sauce, a firm favourite with my family, which I'm sure will become a staple in your repertoire once you try it.

3 tablespoons coconut oil or good-quality animal fat*

16 raw tiger prawns, peeled and deveined, head and tail left intact (see Note)

sea salt and freshly ground black pepper

5 garlic cloves, finely chopped

2 small French shallots, finely chopped

2 long red chillies, deseeded and finely chopped

2 jalapeño chillies, deseeded and finely chopped

1 teaspoon ground cumin

2 large handfuls of coriander leaves and stalks, finely chopped

1 tablespoon lime juice

1 tablespoon orange juice

80 ml (⅓ cup) extra-virgin olive oil

* See Glossary

Heat 1 tablespoon of the coconut oil or fat in a large, heavy-based frying pan over medium–high heat. Add the prawns and cook for 1–1½ minutes on each side until golden and almost cooked through. Season with salt and pepper. Remove the prawns from the pan and set aside, keeping warm.

Reduce the heat to medium and add the remaining oil or fat and the garlic, shallot and red and jalapeño chillies to the pan. Cook, stirring occasionally, for 3 minutes, or until softened. Return the prawns to the pan, add the cumin and coriander and toss through for 30 seconds. Stir in the lime and orange juices and olive oil and season to taste with a little salt and pepper.

Arrange the mojo prawns on a platter and serve.

NOTE If you prefer, you can leave the shells intact and devein the prawns by pulling out the track from the back of the prawn where the tail starts using a skewer. If you leave the shells on, you'll need to cook the prawns for an extra 30 seconds on each side. Doing this will make them even more juicy and flavoursome, though it can be a little fiddly. And remember that you can always eat the shell, head, tail and all, if you like.

CAULIFLOWER AND PUMPKIN DAL WITH TURMERIC FISH

When it comes to comfort food, we often think of stews or braises, rarely fish. Here is a perfect example of comfort food, where fish is the star and nourishing, warming cauliflower and pumpkin are the support acts. This dish is great for those nights when it is cold outside, but you still want to keep things light and simple.

4 x 160 g white fish fillets (barramundi, bream, mulloway, whiting or snapper), skin on, pin-boned
2 tablespoons melted coconut oil or good-quality animal fat*
½ teaspoon ground turmeric
1 bunch of English spinach (about 200 g), trimmed
olive oil, for drizzling
1 handful of coriander leaves
lemon wedges, to serve

CAULIFLOWER AND PUMPKIN DAL
2 tablespoons coconut oil or good-quality animal fat*
1 onion, finely chopped
1 tablespoon finely grated ginger
2 garlic cloves, chopped
500 g butternut pumpkin, peeled and cut into 1 cm cubes
3 teaspoons garam masala
2 teaspoons ground turmeric
2 teaspoons ground cumin
1–2 pinches of cayenne pepper
15 fresh curry leaves
500 ml (2 cups) Chicken Bone Broth (page 246) or water, plus extra if needed
200 ml coconut cream
1 tablespoon lemon juice
600 g (3 ⅓ cups) uncooked Cauliflower Rice (page 246)
sea salt and freshly ground black pepper

* See Glossary

To make the cauliflower and pumpkin dal, heat the coconut oil or fat in a large frying pan over medium heat. Add the onion and sauté for 5 minutes, or until softened. Add the ginger, garlic and pumpkin and cook for 1 minute, then stir in the spices and curry leaves and cook for 30 seconds, or until fragrant.

Pour in the broth or water, coconut cream and lemon juice, cover with a lid and bring to the boil. Reduce the heat to low and simmer for 10 minutes, or until the pumpkin is tender. Stir in the cauliflower rice, cover and simmer for a further 10–15 minutes or until the cauliflower is cooked through, adding a little extra broth or water if needed. Season with salt and pepper.

Meanwhile, preheat the oven to 170°C (150°C fan-forced). Line a baking tray with baking paper.

Coat the fish with the coconut oil or fat, sprinkle the turmeric over the flesh and season with salt and pepper. Heat a large, non-stick frying pan over medium–high heat. Add the fish, skin-side down, and cook for 2 minutes, or until golden and crisp. Transfer the fish to the prepared tray and roast for 6–8 minutes until cooked through. Transfer to a plate and rest for 2 minutes, keeping warm.

Bring a saucepan of salted water to the boil. Add the spinach and cook for 2 minutes, or until tender. Remove with a slotted spoon and place in a bowl, then drizzle over some olive oil and give it a good toss. Season with salt and pepper if needed.

Spoon the cauliflower and pumpkin dal into serving bowls, add the spinach and top with the fish. Scatter over the coriander leaves and serve with the lemon wedges.

SPICED CHICKEN WITH EGGPLANT KASUNDI

I don't think the humble roast chook ever gets old – there are so many ways to elevate it to new heights. Once you start experimenting with flavours, you open up so many possibilities. Here is a simple but delicious roast chook that draws on Indian flavours. You'll need to begin this recipe a day ahead.

4 chicken marylands
2 tablespoons melted coconut oil or good-quality
   animal fat*
1 large handful of coriander sprigs
mixed salad leaves, to serve
lemon cheeks, to serve

SPICED MARINADE
3 teaspoons coriander seeds
2 teaspoons cumin seeds
1½ teaspoons garam masala
2 long green chillies, deseeded and finely chopped
2 teaspoons finely grated ginger
2 garlic cloves
1 tablespoon lemon juice
1 handful of coriander leaves, chopped
80 ml (⅓ cup) melted lard* or duck fat

EGGPLANT KASUNDI
sea salt and freshly ground black pepper
700 g eggplant, cut into 2 cm cubes
1 tablespoon cumin seeds
1 teaspoon mustard seeds
¼ teaspoon fenugreek seeds
1 teaspoon ground turmeric
1 tablespoon finely grated garlic
1 tablespoon finely grated ginger
3 tablespoons melted coconut oil
1 large onion, finely chopped
2 long red chillies, deseeded and finely chopped
100 ml apple cider vinegar
2 tablespoons honey (optional)
10 fresh curry leaves

YOGHURT SAUCE
100 g coconut yoghurt
1 tablespoon lemon juice, or to taste
a pinch of toasted cumin seeds

* See Glossary

To make the spiced marinade, combine the coriander and cumin seeds in a frying pan over medium heat and toast for 1 minute, or until fragrant. Set aside to cool, then grind with a mortar and pestle (or use a spice grinder). Place the ground spices in a food processor, add the remaining spiced marinade ingredients and blend to form a smooth paste. Transfer to a large bowl, add the chicken and turn to coat. Cover and refrigerate overnight.

To start on the kasundi, sprinkle 1 tablespoon of salt over the eggplant, toss well and set aside for 1 hour. Rinse under cold water and pat dry with paper towel.

Next, combine the cumin, mustard and fenugreek seeds in a frying pan and toast over medium heat for 1 minute, or until fragrant. Set aside to cool, then grind with a mortar and pestle (or use a spice grinder). Mix the ground spices with the turmeric, garlic and ginger and add 2 tablespoons of water to form a paste.

Heat 2 tablespoons of the coconut oil in a large frying pan over medium heat. Add the onion and sauté for 5 minutes, or until softened. Add the chilli and the spice paste and cook, stirring frequently, for a further 2 minutes, or until fragrant. Stir in the vinegar, honey (if using) and curry leaves, add the eggplant and the remaining oil and gently stir. Reduce the heat to low and simmer, stirring occasionally, for 30 minutes, or until the eggplant is very soft. Season with salt and pepper. Allow to cool.

Preheat the oven to 180°C (160°C fan-forced).

Brush the chicken with the coconut oil or fat, season with salt and pepper and place in a roasting tin. Roast for 45–55 minutes, turning halfway through, until golden and cooked through.

To make the yoghurt sauce, place the yoghurt and lemon juice in a bowl, add a pinch of salt and mix well. Transfer to a small bowl and sprinkle over the cumin seeds.

Place the chicken on a large platter, pour over the juices from the tin and sprinkle on the coriander sprigs. Serve with the kasundi, yoghurt sauce, salad leaves and lemon cheeks on the side.

SOUTHERN FRIED CHICKEN LIVERS

If you haven't tried crumbed chicken livers, you are in for a real treat – the crunchy spicy crumbs are the perfect coating for the just-cooked livers. Add hot sauce to the mix and you may just become addicted to this dish. Don't say I didn't warn you.

4 eggs
2 tablespoons almond milk
150 g tapioca flour*
800 g chicken livers
coconut oil or good-quality animal fat,*
   for deep-frying
80 ml (⅓ cup) Hot Sauce (page 251)
lemon wedges, to serve

SPICE MIX
3 tablespoons psyllium husks*
3 tablespoons tapioca flour*
200 g (2 cups) almond meal
2 teaspoons dried oregano
2 teaspoons dried mixed herbs
½ teaspoon chilli powder
2 teaspoons freshly ground black pepper
2 teaspoons sea salt
1½ teaspoons sweet paprika
2 teaspoons ground cumin
2 teaspoons garlic powder
2 teaspoons onion powder

* See Glossary

Place all the spice mix ingredients in a shallow bowl and mix well. Whisk the eggs and almond milk in another shallow bowl. Place the tapioca flour in a third bowl.

Rinse the chicken livers under cold water and pat dry with paper towel. Trim off any fat, sinew and veins.

One at a time, toss the chicken livers in the tapioca flour and dust off the excess. Then dip in the egg mixture, followed by the spice mixture, turning and pressing gently to coat thoroughly.

Add enough coconut oil or fat to fill a large saucepan to one-third full and heat to 170°C over medium–high heat. (To test, drop a small piece of chicken liver into the oil; if it starts to bubble around the edges immediately, the oil is ready.) Add the chicken livers in batches and fry for 3 minutes, or until the livers are golden and cooked through. Remove with a slotted spoon and drain on paper towel.

Season the chicken livers with salt and serve with the hot sauce and lemon wedges on the side.

PORTUGUESE CHICKEN

The goal with cooking any dish is to make it as tasty as possible for everyone who eats it. You will notice that theme is in all my books – I prioritise taste and health equally, without sacrificing one for the other. I do hope you love this Portuguese-inspired chicken dish that is full of both flavour and goodness.

1.5 kg chicken drumsticks
freshly ground black pepper
lemon wedges, to serve

MARINADE
4 garlic cloves, finely chopped
2 tablespoons melted lard
1 tablespoon chopped flat-leaf parsley leaves
2 teaspoons finely chopped oregano leaves
1½ teaspoons smoked paprika
finely grated zest and juice of 1 lemon
1 teaspoon ground cumin
1 long red chilli, deseeded and chopped (leave the seeds in if you like it spicy)
1 teaspoon sea salt

PIRI-PIRI SAUCE
2 tablespoons lard or good-quality animal fat*
2 tablespoons sweet paprika
1 tablespoon ground cumin
1 tablespoon ground coriander
1 red capsicum, deseeded and chopped
½ onion, chopped
2 garlic cloves, chopped
3 small red chillies, deseeded and roughly chopped (leave the seeds in if you like it hot)
1 teaspoon grated ginger
3 tablespoons lemon juice
150 ml extra-virgin olive oil

* See Glossary

Combine all the marinade ingredients in a blender and whiz until they form a thick paste (or you can leave it chunkier if you prefer).

Place the chicken in a large bowl. Pour over the marinade and toss well to coat, then season with pepper. Cover and refrigerate for at least 1 hour or, for best results, overnight.

Preheat the oven to 200°C (180°C fan-forced). Grease a large roasting tin.

Transfer the chicken and marinade to the prepared tin. Roast for 30 minutes, flip the chicken over and roast for another 15 minutes, or until the chicken is deep golden brown and the juices run clear when the thickest part is pierced with a skewer.

Meanwhile, to make the piri-piri sauce, combine the lard or fat, paprika, cumin and coriander in a frying pan over medium heat and cook for 10 seconds, or until fragrant. Add the capsicum, onion, garlic, chilli and ginger and sauté for 5 minutes, or until the onion is softened. Stir in 180 ml of water and bring to the boil. Reduce the heat to low and simmer for 10 minutes, or until the sauce has reduced by three-quarters. Allow to cool, then mix in the lemon juice. Transfer the mixture to a blender and whiz until smooth. With the motor running, pour in the olive oil in a slow, steady stream and blend until incorporated. Season with salt and pepper.

Place the chicken on a platter, drizzle over the piri-piri sauce and serve with the lemon wedges on the side.

SPICY PORK LARB

I have shared many larb recipes over the years and I will keep sharing them as larb is one of my go-to dishes when I need flavour but don't have a lot of time to spare. You can have this on the table in 15 minutes, and you can pretty well use any mince that takes your fancy, although pork mince – so fatty and full of flavour – is my favourite.

2 tablespoons coconut oil or good-quality
    animal fat*
2 garlic cloves, finely chopped
1 lemongrass stem, pale part only, finely chopped
600 g pork mince
80 ml (⅓ cup) lime juice
2 tablespoons fish sauce, plus extra if needed
1–2 bird's eye chillies, deseeded and finely chopped
2 kaffir lime leaves, finely chopped
1 spring onion, finely sliced
1 handful of mint leaves
1 handful of coriander leaves
1 small handful of Thai basil leaves
2 red Asian shallots, finely sliced
8 savoy cabbage leaves, trimmed into cups
1 Lebanese cucumber, sliced
100 g Crispy Pork Crackling (page 247), chopped
lime cheeks, to serve

* See Glossary

Heat the coconut oil or fat in a large, heavy-based frying pan over medium–high heat. Add the garlic and lemongrass and stir-fry for 30 seconds, or until fragrant. Add the mince and cook, stirring with a wooden spoon to break up the lumps, for 6 minutes, or until browned and crumbly. Stir in the lime juice, fish sauce, chilli, lime leaves and spring onion. Remove from the heat and leave to cool for 1 minute.

Toss half the mint, coriander, Thai basil and shallot through the mince. Taste and add a little more fish sauce if needed.

Spoon into the cabbage cups and add the cucumber, then scatter over the pork crackling, the remaining herbs and shallot. Serve with lime cheeks on the side.

MEXICAN LAMB WITH ROAST PUMPKIN

Stuffing vegetables isn't anything new; in fact, I can remember Mum stuffing mushrooms and capsicums when I was a youngster and it was all the rage a few decades ago. These days I like to roast larger vegetables, such as sweet potato, pumpkin, cabbage and cauliflower, and team them with some delicious meat or seafood to create a complete meal. If you are following a strict keto diet, then perhaps use mushrooms or zucchini instead of pumpkin, or eat the lamb with lettuce or cabbage cups. If you're cycling out of ketosis, this recipe is perfect for you.

1 butternut pumpkin (1.8–2 kg), halved lengthways, deseeded
2 tablespoons melted coconut oil or good-quality animal fat*
1 handful of coriander sprigs
extra-virgin olive oil, for drizzling
1 lime, halved

MEXICAN LAMB

2 tablespoons coconut oil or good-quality animal fat*
2 onions, finely chopped
4 garlic cloves, finely chopped
500 ml (2 cups) Beef Bone Broth (page 245)
400 g whole peeled tomatoes (see Note page 86)
1 tablespoon chipotle chillies in adobo sauce
sea salt and freshly ground black pepper
1 tablespoon Mexican spice blend
2 teaspoons ground cumin
1 x 2.3 kg lamb shoulder, bone in, fat scored, at room temperature

GUACAMOLE

2 avocados, diced
½ small red onion, finely chopped
1 long red chilli, deseeded and finely chopped
1 tablespoon finely chopped coriander leaves
2 tablespoons lime juice, or to taste
3 tablespoons olive oil

* See Glossary

Preheat the oven to 110°C (90°C fan-forced).

To start on the Mexican lamb, heat the coconut oil or fat in a saucepan over medium–high heat. Add the onion and sauté for 5–8 minutes until caramelised. Stir in the garlic and sauté for a further 2 minutes, or until starting to colour. Add the broth, tomatoes and chipotle chillies in adobo sauce and bring to the boil. Remove from the heat and season with salt and pepper.

Rub the Mexican spice blend, cumin and a generous amount of salt and pepper into the scored flesh of the lamb. Place the lamb, fat-side up, in a casserole dish, pour over the tomato and onion mixture and cover with a lid. Braise in the oven for 8–10 hours until the meat pulls away easily from the bone. If there is any resistance, braise for a little longer.

Remove the lamb from the dish, reserving the liquid. Place the dish over medium heat and reduce the liquid until it has thickened enough to coat the back of a spoon. Slice or shred the lamb and add 250 ml of the reduced liquid to moisten. Season with more salt and pepper if needed.

Increase the oven temperature to 180°C (160°C fan-forced).

Brush the pumpkin with the melted coconut oil or fat. Place, cut-side up, in a roasting tin and sprinkle with salt and pepper. Roast for 1¼–1½ hours until tender.

Place all the guacamole ingredients in a bowl, season with salt and pepper and mix to combine. Set aside.

Place the roast pumpkin halves on a platter and top with the lamb. Sprinkle over the coriander, drizzle on some olive oil and serve with the lime halves and guacamole.

THAI RED CURRY WITH BRAISED LAMB SHANKS

I have been a massive admirer of red curries for a few decades now, ever since I tried one on my first trip to Thailand, as they work well with strong flavours like lamb, beef, goat, duck and other game meats. If you are looking for something super nourishing and comforting, then the ever-popular lamb shanks work a treat, with the addition of vegetables to build flavour and texture. These days you can purchase really good red curry pastes that don't have any nasties, or you can make your own, which is really very satisfying.

80 ml (⅓ cup) melted coconut oil or good-quality animal fat*
4 lamb shanks (about 450 g each)
sea salt and freshly ground black pepper
1 onion, chopped
3 garlic cloves, chopped
3 tablespoons Thai red curry paste
600 ml coconut cream
250 ml (1 cup) Chicken Bone Broth (page 246)
1 sweet potato, cut into 2.5 cm pieces
2 zucchini, thickly sliced
1 head of broccoli (about 300 g), broken into florets
1 tablespoon fish sauce
2 teaspoons monk fruit sweetener* (optional)
1 teaspoon lime juice
1 large handful each of coriander and Thai basil leaves
360 g (2 cups) cooked Cauliflower Rice (page 246)

* See Glossary

Preheat the oven to 150°C (130°C fan-forced).

Rub some of the coconut oil or fat into the lamb shanks and season with salt and pepper.

Heat half the remaining oil or fat in a large, flameproof casserole dish over medium–high heat. Add the lamb shanks in two batches and sear for 5 minutes on all sides until well browned. Place the shanks on a plate and set aside.

Reduce the heat to medium, add the remaining oil or fat and the onion and sauté for 5 minutes, or until the onion is softened. Stir in the garlic and curry paste and cook for 1 minute, or until fragrant. Pour in the coconut cream and broth, return the lamb shanks to the dish and bring to the boil.

Cover the dish with a lid and transfer to the oven. Braise, turning occasionally, for 2 hours, or until the lamb is almost tender. Add the sweet potato and stir, then cover and cook for 30 minutes.

Stir the zucchini and broccoli into the curry and continue to braise, uncovered, for a further 30 minutes, or until the meat is falling off the bone and the vegetables are tender. Add the fish sauce, monk fruit sweetener (if using) and lime juice and taste. There should be a pronounced tartness with a balance of sweetness – adjust the seasoning if necessary.

Sprinkle over the coriander and Thai basil leaves and serve with the cauliflower rice.

KOREAN-SPICED LAMB CHOPS WITH BEAN SPROUTS

I grew up loving lamb chops, and I still love them to this day. The wonderful thing about them is their delicious amount of healthy fat. Plus, they don't take too long to cook, and their intense flavour is easy to enhance. In this recipe I've spiced them up Korean style – once you taste them, you will make them time and time again.

8 x lamb loin chops
2 tablespoons coconut oil or good-quality
   animal fat*
2 tablespoons Typhoon Garlic (page 257)
1 spring onion, green part only, sliced diagonally

MARINADE
3 tablespoons tamari or coconut aminos*
2 tablespoons honey (optional)
1 tablespoon finely grated ginger
4 garlic cloves, grated
1 tablespoon toasted sesame oil
¼ teaspoon Korean chilli powder (gochugaru)*
   or chilli powder
1 tablespoon Sriracha Chilli Sauce (page 256)
1 tablespoon apple cider vinegar

SEASONED BEAN SPROUTS
2 tablespoons coconut oil or good-quality
   animal fat*
250 g bean sprouts, rinsed and drained well
1½ tablespoons tamari or coconut aminos*
1 teaspoon honey (optional)
1 teaspoon sesame seeds
sea salt and freshly ground black pepper

* See Glossary

Place all the marinade ingredients in a large, shallow bowl and mix well. Add the lamb chops and turn to coat. Cover and refrigerate for at least 2 hours or, for best results, overnight.

To make the seasoned bean sprouts, heat the coconut oil or fat in a large frying pan over medium heat. Add the bean sprouts and cook for 2–3 minutes until heated through. Add the tamari or coconut aminos, honey (if using) and sesame seeds and cook for a further minute. Remove from the pan and set aside to allow the flavours to develop.

Heat a barbecue grill plate to medium–hot or place a chargrill pan over medium–high heat and brush with the coconut oil or fat. Shake the marinade off the chops and reserve.

Cook the chops for 3 minutes on each side for medium–rare, or cook to your liking. Place the chops on a plate, and rest for 3 minutes, keeping warm.

Pour the reserved marinade into a saucepan and simmer over medium heat for 2–3 minutes until the sauce has thickened.

Divide the lamb chops among serving plates and add the seasoned bean sprouts. Sprinkle over the typhoon garlic and spring onion and serve with the sauce.

CHILLI BEEF FAJITA WITH SWEET POTATO WEDGES

A traditional fajita is simply meat, usually spiced or marinated, that is grilled over a fire or in a pan and served in a tortilla. In this recipe I have swapped out the tortilla for some sweet potato wedges, as I love that combination – and it's easier too. If you want to stay in ketosis, replace the sweet potato with lettuce or cabbage cups. If you are cycling in and out (as I do) and feel like a change, substitute pumpkin for the sweet potato. The key here is the delicious sauce and spice combination that works so well with the beef.

3 sweet potatoes (about 800 g), cut into
   2.5 cm wedges
100 ml melted coconut oil or good-quality
   animal fat*
sea salt and freshly ground black pepper
700 g beef sirloin or tri-tip, fat and sinew removed,
   cut into strips
juice of ½ lime, plus extra to serve
½ teaspoon ground cumin
1 teaspoon smoked paprika
2 teaspoons chipotle chillies in adobo sauce
1 onion, sliced
1 red capsicum, deseeded and sliced
4 garlic cloves, finely chopped
400 g diced tomatoes (see Note page 86)
1 handful of coriander sprigs
lime wedges, to serve

* See Glossary

Preheat the oven to 200°C (180°C fan-forced). Lightly grease a large baking tray.

Place the sweet potato wedges in a bowl, add 2 tablespoons of the coconut oil or fat and some salt and pepper and mix well. Spread the wedges out on the prepared tray in a single layer. Roast for about 20 minutes, then turn the wedges over and roast for another 20 minutes, or until tender and golden.

Meanwhile, place the beef strips, lime juice, spices and chipotle chillies in adobo sauce in a non-reactive bowl and season with salt and pepper. Toss the meat to coat. Cover and marinate at room temperature for 15 minutes.

Heat 2 tablespoons of the oil or fat in a heavy-based frying pan over medium–high heat. Add the onion and sauté for 3 minutes, or until softened. Add the capsicum and sauté for 5 minutes, or until slightly softened. Stir in the garlic and sauté for 30 seconds, or until fragrant. Pour in the tomatoes and 120 ml of water. Reduce the heat to medium–low and simmer for 15 minutes. Season to taste with salt and pepper.

Heat the remaining oil or fat in a large, heavy-based frying pan over medium–high heat. Add the marinated beef strips in batches and sauté for 2 minutes until slightly charred and medium–rare, or cook to your liking. Add the vegetable mixture and mix to combine.

Scatter the coriander sprigs over the chilli beef and serve with the sweet potato and lime wedges.

ROAST AND BAKED

HULI HULI CHICKEN WINGS

Sweet, smoky and tangy, these chicken wings get their flavour from an easy-to-make Hawaiian marinade. They're as great for a weekend get-together with friends as they are on any weeknight for the whole family. The thing I love most? These wings are finger-licking good. Just remember that this dish is for higher carb days due to the pineapple in the marinade.

1.8 kg chicken wings
1 handful of coriander sprigs
lime halves, to serve

MARINADE
300 g pineapple, chopped
100 ml tamari or coconut aminos*
100 g Tomato Ketchup (page 257)
2 tablespoons apple cider vinegar
3 tablespoons finely grated ginger
3 garlic cloves, finely chopped
3 tablespoons honey (optional)
2 teaspoons sweet paprika
2 teaspoons ground cumin
1½ teaspoons onion powder
½ teaspoon chilli powder
2 tablespoons melted lard* or coconut oil

* See Glossary

To make the marinade, place the pineapple, tamari or coconut aminos, tomato ketchup and vinegar in a high-speed blender and whiz until smooth. Strain the liquid through a fine sieve into a large bowl, pressing down with a spoon to remove as much liquid as possible; discard the pulp. Add the ginger, garlic, honey (if using), paprika, cumin, onion powder, chilli powder and lard and mix to combine.

Add the chicken wings to the marinade and turn to coat. Cover and refrigerate for at least 1 hour or, for best results, overnight.

Preheat the oven to 200°C (180°C fan-forced).

Transfer the chicken and marinade to a large roasting tin and spread out in a single layer. Roast, turning the wings occasionally, for 40–45 minutes until the chicken is a lovely golden brown and cooked through.

Arrange the chicken wings on a serving platter and pour over any juices in the tin. Scatter over the coriander sprigs and serve with the lime halves on the side.

LEMON-MYRTLE ROAST CHICKEN

I am truly grateful that I grew up in a household that loved a roast chook. Fast forward to now, and roast chicken is something I love to feed my own kids. Here is Mum's recipe, with a little twist in the form of some delicious and uniquely Australian lemon myrtle. Thanks, Mum, for nourishing me with the most delicious roasts, and starting a tradition I continue to this day.

4 chicken marylands
3 tablespoons melted coconut oil or good-quality
    animal fat*
4 garlic cloves, finely grated
1 tablespoon ground lemon myrtle
2 fresh bay leaves
sea salt and freshly ground black pepper
2 lemons, thickly sliced
650 ml Chicken Jus (page 247)
1 tablespoon finely chopped oregano leaves

* See Glossary

Place the chicken in a large, shallow bowl, smear on the coconut oil or fat, then scatter over the garlic, lemon myrtle and bay leaves and season with salt and pepper. Toss to coat the chicken, then cover and refrigerate for 1 hour.

Preheat the oven to 200°C (180°C fan-forced). Lightly grease a roasting tin.

Place the chicken in the prepared tin, scatter the lemon slices around the chicken and roast, basting occasionally with the juices in the tin, for 45–50 minutes until the chicken is golden and the juices run clear when a leg is pierced with a skewer.

Place the chicken jus in a saucepan and bring to a simmer to ensure it is heated through.

Transfer the chicken and lemon slices to a platter, sprinkle over the oregano and serve with the warm chicken jus.

HONEY-SOY CHICKEN WINGS

If someone mentions chicken wings, it stops me in my tracks. Once considered a poor cousin to the thigh or breast, these days wings appear on restaurant menus the world over. I love that they suit every cuisine you can think of – South American, Portuguese, French, Italian, American, Mexican, Asian – and that we can create countless recipes to suit each and every one. Here is my version of the first chicken wing dish I ever tried and, from the first bite to the last lick of my fingers, I knew we were in for a wonderful culinary relationship. This recipe is only suitable for higher carb days due to the honey in the marinade.

12 chicken wings
2 teaspoons sesame seeds, toasted
2 limes, halved

MARINADE
4 garlic cloves, finely chopped
1 tablespoon finely grated ginger
100 g honey
½ teaspoon Chinese five spice
100 ml tamari or coconut aminos*
2 tablespoons shaoxing wine or dry sherry
1 tablespoon melted coconut oil or good-quality
  animal fat*

* See Glossary

Combine all the marinade ingredients in a large, shallow bowl. Add the chicken wings to the marinade and toss to coat well. Cover and refrigerate for at least 2 hours or, for best results, overnight.

Preheat the oven to 200°C (180°C fan-forced).

Place the chicken wings in a roasting tin and pour over the marinade. Roast for 30 minutes, then flip the wings over and continue to roast for another 15 minutes, or until the chicken is completely cooked through and dark golden brown.

Take the tray out of the oven and pour the juices into a small saucepan. Place over medium heat and reduce for 5 minutes or until slightly thickened.

Use a pastry brush to brush the chicken all over with the glaze. Transfer to a platter, sprinkle over the sesame seeds and serve with the lime halves.

SHORT RIB AND KIDNEY PIE

Eating nose to tail can dramatically improve our health. Kidneys are chock-full of iron and vitamin B12, and this pie is a great way to enjoy them. You can start by adding a small amount, then gradually increase it.

80 ml (⅓ cup) melted coconut oil or good-quality animal fat*

1.3 kg boneless short ribs, cut into 3 cm cubes

500 g veal kidneys, trimmed and cut into 3 cm pieces

sea salt and freshly ground black pepper

2 onions, finely chopped

2 carrots, finely chopped

4 garlic cloves, finely chopped

3 tablespoons tomato paste

200 ml red wine (such as shiraz)

300 ml Beef Bone Broth (page 245)

400 g diced tomatoes (see Note page 86)

2 tablespoons Worcestershire sauce

1½ teaspoons thyme leaves

3 fresh bay leaves

200 g portobello mushrooms, chopped

2 tablespoons tapioca flour* mixed with 3 tablespoons of water

1 egg

PASTRY

95 g (scant 1 cup) almond meal, sifted

75 g (¾ cup) coconut flour, sifted

60 g (½ cup) tapioca flour*

¾ teaspoon fine sea salt

180 g lard,* chilled, cut into 2.5 cm cubes

65 ml ice-cold water

1 teaspoon apple cider vinegar

1 egg

* See Glossary

Preheat the oven to 130°C (110°C fan-forced).

Heat 2 tablespoons of the oil or fat in a flameproof casserole dish over high heat. Season the short rib and kidney with salt and pepper. Add the short rib in batches and sear for 2–3 minutes on each side. Next, add the kidneys and sear for 1–2 minutes. Set aside. Heat 1 tablespoon of the oil or fat in the dish, add the onion, carrot and garlic and sauté over medium heat for 10 minutes until tender. Stir in the tomato paste and cook for 1 minute. Add the wine, broth, tomatoes, Worcestershire sauce, thyme and bay leaves and bring to the boil. Return the meat and kidney to the dish, cover with a lid and braise in the oven for 3 hours, or until the meat is meltingly soft.

Heat the remaining oil or fat in a heavy-based saucepan over medium–high heat, add the mushroom and fry for 5–6 minutes until golden. Season with salt and pepper, then add to the braised meat and kidney mixture. Whisk through the tapioca paste to thicken and season to taste, if needed. Allow to cool.

To make the pastry, combine the almond meal, coconut flour, tapioca flour and salt in a large bowl. Using your fingertips, gently rub the lard in until the mixture resembles fine crumbs. In a separate bowl, whisk together the water, vinegar and egg. Pour over the dry ingredients and mix to form a soft and slightly sticky dough. Turn the dough out onto a clean surface and shape into a ball. Cover and chill in the fridge for at least 1 hour.

Preheat the oven to 180°C (160°C fan-forced).

To make an egg wash, place the egg and 2 tablespoons of water in a bowl, add a pinch of salt and whisk to combine. Set aside.

Roll out the dough between two sheets of baking paper to 5 mm thick. Transfer to a tray and freeze for 10 minutes to firm up. Remove the pastry from the freezer and peel off the top layer of paper. Carefully flip over and place the pastry, paper-side up, on top of the casserole dish. Run your fingers around the edge to seal, then peel away the paper. Trim any overhanging pastry and crimp the edges with a fork. If there are any cracks, use your fingers to bind the pastry together. Make an incision in the pastry by inserting a knife into the centre. Brush over the egg wash and season with salt.

Bake for 30–35 minutes until the pastry is golden and the filling is hot.

SMOKY PORK RIBS

Ribs are so popular these days that you can pretty much go to any major city and find a ribs restaurant to satisfy your cravings. I have kept this recipe simple and authentic, but have also packed it with as much flavour as possible so you won't need to go to any restaurant once you master it. I guarantee your friends and family members will ask you for the recipe or beg you to cook these ribs for them again.

2 x American-style pork rib racks (about 1.2 kg in total)
100 g lard*
2 tablespoons coconut oil or good-quality animal fat*
200 g Smoky Barbecue Sauce (page 255)

BARBECUE SPICE RUB
1 tablespoon sea salt
2 tablespoons smoked paprika
2 teaspoons freshly ground black pepper
1 tablespoon onion powder
1 tablespoon garlic powder

* See Glossary

Preheat the oven to 140°C (120°C fan-forced).

Combine the barbecue spice rub ingredients in a small bowl.

Coat the ribs with the lard. Smear 2 tablespoons of the barbecue spice rub evenly over the ribs.

Heat a barbecue hotplate to hot or a place large, heavy-based frying pan over high heat and brush with the coconut oil or fat. Seal the ribs for 2 minutes on each side until browned.

Place the ribs in a large casserole dish, add 250 ml of water and cover tightly with baking paper and a lid. Place the ribs in the oven and roast for 3 hours, or until tender.

Increase the oven temperature to 220°C (200°C fan-forced).

Baste the ribs with the smoky barbecue sauce and roast, uncovered, for 15 minutes, or until the glaze is caramelised. Serve immediately with plenty of serviettes.

NOTE You can store the remaining barbecue spice rub in an airtight container in the pantry for up to 6 months.

SWEET POTATO FILLED WITH PULLED PORK

Many people like to cycle in and out of ketosis for long-term sustainable health. This is how I love to eat pulled pork on the days when I am breaking out of ketosis and eating a few more carbs. Of course, if you are following a keto diet for medical reasons, the sweet potato may not be right for you. You could instead pair your pulled pork with coleslaw, spaghetti squash, zucchini or eggplant; roast mushroom or capsicum; or even lettuce or cabbage cups.

3 tablespoons melted coconut oil or good-quality animal fat*
1.5 kg boneless pork shoulder, skin removed, halved
sea salt and freshly ground black pepper
3 tablespoons maple syrup
1½ tablespoons garlic powder
1½ tablespoons onion powder
125 g (½ cup) Smoky Barbecue Sauce (page 255)
3 tablespoons Worcestershire sauce
6 small sweet potatoes (about 1.3 kg in total)

CABBAGE AND CARROT SLAW
500 g cabbage (about ¼ cabbage), shredded
2 carrots, grated
1 red onion, finely sliced
1 handful of coriander leaves, finely chopped, plus extra coriander leaves to serve
125 g (½ cup) Mayonnaise (page 252)
finely grated zest and juice of 1 lemon
1 garlic clove, finely chopped

* See Glossary

Preheat the oven to 110°C (90°C fan-forced). Lightly grease a roasting tin.

Rub 1 tablespoon of the coconut oil or fat into the pork. Season with salt and pepper.

Heat the remaining oil or fat in a large, heavy-based frying pan over high heat. Add the pork halves and sear for 2 minutes on all sides until lightly browned. Transfer the pork, fat-side up, to the prepared tin.

Mix the maple syrup, garlic powder, onion powder, barbecue sauce, Worcestershire sauce and 500 ml of water in a bowl. Pour over the pork, cover the tin tightly with a double layer of foil and roast for 9–10 hours until the pork is very tender. Remove the pork, reserving the liquid. Slice or shred the pork, adding 3 tablespoons of the reserved liquid to moisten. Season with more salt and pepper if needed.

Pour the remaining liquid into a heavy-based saucepan and place over medium–high heat. Simmer for 10–15 minutes or until the sauce has thickened enough to coat the back of a spoon. Set aside, keeping warm.

Increase the oven temperature to 180°C (160°C fan-forced).

Prick the sweet potatoes a few times with a fork. Place on a baking tray and roast for 1 hour, or until tender.

To make the cabbage and carrot slaw, place the cabbage, carrot, onion and coriander in a bowl and gently mix. Place the mayonnaise, lemon zest and juice and garlic in a separate bowl, season to taste and mix well. Add to the cabbage mixture and gently toss.

To serve, cut the sweet potatoes almost in half lengthways. Do not cut all the way through. Slightly open up the cut centre on each sweet potato, fill with the pulled pork, drizzle over the reduced sauce and top with the slaw and some extra coriander leaves.

GLAZED ROAST PORK BUTT WITH APPLE SAUCE

Despite its colourful name, pork butt does not come from anywhere near the rear end of the pig. In fact, quite the opposite. Pork butt is a cut of meat from the shoulder, and it is typically used in pulled pork dishes. It can be roasted or cut into steaks, but it is also well suited to stews, braises and curries. Pork butt is relatively inexpensive, so speak to your butcher about getting some to try out. You will love this recipe on days when you want to increase your carb content slightly to break out of ketosis.

2 red onions, thickly sliced

1.7 kg pork butt, rolled and tied

80 ml (⅓ cup) coconut oil or good-quality animal fat*

sea salt and freshly ground black pepper

800 g kent pumpkin, cut into thick wedges

2 carrots, cut into large chunks

1 garlic bulb, halved horizontally

6 French shallots, cut into wedges

a few thyme sprigs

Pork Jus (page 255), to serve

HONEY-GLAZE MARINADE

100 g honey

6 garlic cloves, finely grated

2 teaspoons sea salt

1 teaspoon smoked paprika

3 tablespoons apple cider vinegar

APPLE SAUCE

1½ tablespoons coconut oil or good-quality animal fat*

3 granny smith apples, peeled, cored and sliced

1½ tablespoons honey (optional)

a pinch of ground cinnamon

1 garlic clove, finely chopped

* See Glossary

Combine all the honey-glaze marinade ingredients in a bowl.

Preheat the oven to 170°C (150°C fan-forced). Grease a roasting tin and a baking tray. Arrange the red onion slices in the tin in a single layer to make a bed for the pork.

Coat the pork with 2 tablespoons of the oil and season generously with salt and pepper. Heat a large frying pan over medium–high heat and seal the pork on all sides for a total of 6–8 minutes or until well browned.

Place the pork on top of the onion in the tin, then brush with the marinade and pour in 125 ml of water. Arrange the pumpkin, carrot, garlic, shallot and thyme on the prepared tray, drizzle over the remaining oil or fat and season with salt and pepper.

Place the pork and veggies in the oven and roast, basting the pork from time to time, for 1½–1¾ hours or until the veggies are tender and the pork is cooked through (the internal temperature of the pork should be 71°C). Cover the pork loosely with foil if it starts to brown too much during cooking.

Meanwhile, to make the apple sauce, melt the coconut oil or fat in a frying pan over medium–low heat. Add the apple and cook, stirring occasionally, for 5–10 minutes. Stir in the honey (if using), cinnamon, garlic and 80 ml of water, then cover and cook, stirring occasionally, for 5 minutes, or until very soft. Mash with a fork or puree with a hand-held blender, then transfer to a serving bowl.

Once the pork is cooked through, transfer to a plate and rest for 15 minutes, keeping warm.

Just before you are ready to serve, place the pork jus in a saucepan and bring to a simmer to heat through. If you'd like to caramelise the veggies a little more, pop them under the grill for a few minutes

Carve the pork and serve with the roast veg, apple sauce and jus.

ROAST PORK BELLY WITH CABBAGE AND HAZELNUTS

Pork and cabbage – like fish and lemon, tomato and basil, steak and onions, pâté and pickles – is a beautiful pairing that has stood the test of time. You could try Asian cabbage with braised pork, duck-fat roasted cabbage with bacon, or make this European-inspired crispy pork belly with cabbage and hazelnuts. It's a super delicious dish.

1 kg boned pork belly, skin scored, at room temperature
250 ml (1 cup) boiling water
1 tablespoon lard*
sea salt
Aioli (page 245), to serve

DRESSING
3 tablespoons sherry vinegar
100 ml extra-virgin olive oil
1 teaspoon Dijon mustard

SALAD
300 g red cabbage, shredded
200 g savoy cabbage, shredded
1 granny smith apple, cut into matchsticks
1 handful of basil leaves
1 handful of chervil leaves
3 tablespoons raisins
80 g hazelnuts (activated if possible),* toasted and chopped

* See Glossary

Preheat the oven to 240°C (220°C fan-forced) – you need to start by blasting the pork with heat.

Place the pork belly on a wire rack in the kitchen sink, carefully pour the boiling water all over the skin, then pat dry with paper towel.

Rub the pork skin with the lard and season generously with salt. Place the pork in a large roasting tin and roast for 35–40 minutes until the skin starts to bubble.

Reduce the temperature to 150°C (130°C fan-forced) and continue to roast for 1 hour, or until the flesh is tender. Transfer to a plate and rest for 15 minutes, keeping warm. If the crackling isn't crisp enough, place the pork, crackling-side up, under a hot grill for a few minutes. Keep a close eye on it under the grill, as the skin can burn very quickly if you leave it too long.

Combine all the dressing ingredients in a small bowl.

Place all the salad ingredients in a large bowl, drizzle over the dressing and gently toss.

Carve the pork into thick slices and serve with the salad and a generous dollop of aioli.

LAMB SHANK SHEPHERD'S PIE WITH PARSNIP AND CAULIFLOWER MASH

SERVES 6

The mere mention of lamb shanks has me salivating, and long, slow cooking of this tasty cut makes for the perfect pie filling. Top with this keto-friendly mash and you have the ultimate winter comfort food.

3 tablespoons coconut oil or good-quality animal fat*

4 lamb shanks (about 450 g each)

sea salt and freshly ground black pepper

2 onions, chopped

4 celery stalks, chopped

4 garlic cloves, crushed

1 teaspoon fresh or dried thyme leaves

2 tablespoons tomato paste

250 ml (1 cup) red wine (such as shiraz)

400 g whole peeled tomatoes, crushed (see Note page 86)

500 ml (2 cups) Beef Bone Broth (page 245) or water

2 tablespoons tapioca flour*

3 tablespoons chopped flat-leaf parsley leaves

PARSNIP AND CAULIFLOWER MASH

1 garlic bulb

3 tablespoons coconut oil or good-quality animal fat*

5 small parsnips (about 450 g in total), peeled and core removed

1 head of cauliflower (about 1 kg), florets cut into 5 cm pieces

2 eggs

* See Glossary

Rub 2 tablespoons of the coconut oil or fat over the lamb shanks and season with salt and pepper. Place a large, flameproof casserole dish over medium–high heat, add the shanks and sear for 4 minutes on all sides until browned. Transfer to a plate and set aside.

Heat the remaining oil or fat in the dish over medium heat, add the onion, celery, garlic and thyme and sauté for 5 minutes, or until the vegetables begin to soften. Stir in the tomato paste and cook for 2 minutes, then pour in the wine and simmer for 5 minutes, or until almost evaporated.

Combine the tomatoes and broth or water in a bowl. Place the tapioca flour in a small bowl and mix in 3 tablespoons of water until smooth. Stir the tapioca paste into the tomato mixture.

Stir the tomato mixture into the dish, return the shanks, ensuring the meaty parts are well submerged, and bring to the boil. Reduce the heat to low, cover with a lid and simmer for 2½–3 hours until the meat is tender and falling off the bone. Stir occasionally to prevent the sauce from catching on the bottom of the dish.

Meanwhile, start on the mash. Preheat the oven to 180°C (160°C fan-forced). Place the garlic on a baking tray and coat with some of the oil or fat. Roast for 35–40 minutes until golden and tender.

Bring a large saucepan of salted water to the boil. Add the parsnip and cauliflower and cook for 15 minutes, or until tender. Drain and shake off any excess water, then place in a food processor. Cut the roasted garlic in half horizontally and squeeze the flesh into the processor. Add the remaining oil or fat, the eggs and 80 ml of water. Process until smooth and season with salt and pepper.

Remove the shanks from the dish. Bring the sauce to a simmer over medium heat and cook, stirring occasionally, for 10–15 minutes until thickened. Shred the meat (reserve the bones) and return to the dish, add the parsley; stir to combine. Taste and season if needed.

Reduce the oven temperature to 180°C (160°C fan-forced).

Spoon the meat filling into a baking dish, then arrange the reserved bones upright in the filling. Spread the mash around the bones to cover the filling. Bake for 30 minutes until the top is golden and the filling is bubbling. Serve with some greens or a fresh salad.

LAMB RIBS WITH RED CHIMICHURRI

I love it when trends make it from restaurants into people's kitchens, and recently lamb ribs have done just that. This recipe is the bomb – the ribs are fatty and deliciously meaty. To really make them come alive, I have teamed them with red chimichurri and preserved lemon. If you can't find lamb ribs, pork or beef ribs or lamb chops will give a similar result, or for something a little different, use lamb mince to make patties.

3 x 600 g racks of lamb ribs, at room temperature
sea salt and freshly ground black pepper
finely chopped preserved lemon rind, to serve

SPICE RUB
2 tablespoons ground cumin
2 tablespoons finely chopped mint leaves
2 tablespoons finely chopped oregano leaves
1 tablespoon smoked paprika
6 garlic cloves
2 teaspoons finely grated lemon zest
100 ml olive oil

RED CHIMICHURRI
1 red capsicum, deseeded and chopped into
   large pieces
2 tomatoes, deseeded and roughly chopped
1 small red onion, roughly chopped
2 very large handfuls of coriander leaves
80 ml (⅓ cup) red wine vinegar, plus extra if needed
1 jalapeño chilli, deseeded and chopped
2 garlic cloves, chopped
1 teaspoon ground cumin
1 teaspoon finely chopped oregano leaves
½ teaspoon smoked paprika
½ teaspoon chilli flakes
125 ml (½ cup) olive oil
1 large handful of flat-leaf parsley leaves,
   finely chopped

Preheat the oven to 130°C (110°C fan-forced).

To make the spice rub, combine the cumin, herbs and paprika in a bowl. Use a mortar and pestle to pound the garlic to a fine paste. Stir in the lemon zest, spice mixture and olive oil. Set aside.

Place the lamb racks on a baking tray and score the meat with a sharp knife. Smear the spice rub over the ribs and season well with salt and pepper. Roast for 3 hours, or until the meat is meltingly tender and falling off the bone.

Meanwhile, place all the red chimichurri ingredients except the parsley in a food processor and process until just finely chopped. Season with salt and pepper. Cover and refrigerate for at least 1 hour to allow the flavours to develop. Transfer to a small serving bowl and mix in the parsley.

Cut each lamb rack into individual ribs and arrange on a platter. Drizzle over some red chimichurri, scatter over the preserved lemon rind and serve with the remaining red chimichurri on the side.

SLOW-COOKED SOUTHERN BRISKET

SERVES 8

On my first visit to southern USA about ten years ago, I was truly blown away by the standard of cooking, the quality of produce and the local chefs' depth of knowledge. One of the meals I got to experience was a proper American slow-cooked brisket barbecue. And, I have to say, it was up there with the best meat I have ever had the pleasure of eating. Serve this with your roast vegetables, salad or slaw.

2 tablespoons melted coconut oil or good-quality animal fat*

1 x 3 kg beef brisket

sea salt and freshly ground black pepper

3 tablespoons Barbecue Spice Rub (page 142)

4 French shallots, unpeeled, halved lengthways

1 garlic bulb, halved horizontally and broken into 8 pieces

8 thyme sprigs

300 ml Beef or Chicken Bone Broth (page 245 or 246)

* See Glossary

Preheat the oven to 100°C (80°C fan-forced).

Rub the coconut oil or fat over the brisket, then lightly season with salt and pepper.

Heat a large roasting tin over high heat, add the brisket and seal on all sides for 3–4 minutes until browned. Place the brisket, fat-side up, on a large plate. When cool enough to handle, evenly coat the sealed brisket with the barbecue spice rub.

Arrange the shallot, garlic and thyme in the tin in a single layer, place the brisket on top and pour in the broth. Cover the brisket firmly with a damp piece of baking paper, then tightly cover the tin with a double layer of foil. Roast for 12 hours, or until the brisket is tender. Place the brisket on a plate, cover loosely and rest for 15–30 minutes, keeping warm.

Thickly carve the brisket and serve.

GRILL

BARBE

AND

STIR-

ED,
CUED
FRIED

BARBECUED PRAWNS WITH AVOCADO AND MANGO

When summer is in full swing, nothing beats prawns on the barbecue with a tropical salad to complement them. And when I say tropical salad, you can use any fruit or vegetable that's in season and bursting with flavour. Here is one of my all-time favourite combinations: ripe mango and avocado with macadamias, mint and a spicy dressing. You could also use pineapple, green papaya, lychees, rambutans, figs or finger limes.

18 raw large king prawns, shelled and deveined, tails left intact
2 tablespoons melted coconut oil or good-quality animal fat*
sea salt and freshly ground black pepper
1 mango, cut into 1.5 cm cubes
1 large handful of mint leaves
1 large handful of Thai basil leaves
2 avocados, cut into 1 cm cubes
80 g (½ cup) macadamia nuts (activated if possible),* toasted and chopped
lime cheeks, to serve

NAM JIM DRESSING
1 red Asian shallot, chopped
2 long red chillies, deseeded and chopped
2 garlic cloves, chopped
2.5 cm piece of ginger, chopped
1 tablespoon finely chopped coriander roots and stalks
150 ml lime juice
2 tablespoons coconut sugar or honey (optional)
2 tablespoons fish sauce

* See Glossary

To make the nam jim dressing, pound the shallot, chilli, garlic, ginger and coriander roots and stalks to a paste using a large mortar and pestle. Add the lime juice and mix well. Stir through the coconut sugar or honey (if using) and fish sauce, taste and adjust the seasoning if necessary, so that the dressing is a balance of hot, sour, salty and sweet.

Heat the barbecue hotplate to hot or place a large, heavy-based frying pan over high heat.

Brush the prawns with the coconut oil or fat and cook for 1–1½ minutes on each side until charred and cooked through. Season with salt and pepper.

Place the mango and herbs in a bowl, pour on half the nam jim dressing and gently toss.

Arrange the mango salad on a platter, then top with the avocado and prawns. Pour over the remaining nam jim dressing, sprinkle over the macadamias and serve with the lime cheeks on the side.

SUMAC SALMON SKEWERS WITH HEMP SEED HUMMUS

The addition of one or two spices can really enhance an ingredient. Take this simple dish, for example: add some sumac, cumin, salt and pepper and, voila, you have superbly spiced salmon. Teamed with hemp seed hummus and a fragrant tabbouleh, this is what good food is all about.

700 g salmon fillet, skin off, pin-boned and cut into
   3 cm cubes
2 tablespoons melted coconut oil or good-quality
   animal fat*
finely grated zest of ½ lemon
1 teaspoon sumac*
½ teaspoon ground cumin

TABBOULEH
¼ red onion, finely chopped
1 garlic clove, finely grated
2 large handfuls of flat-leaf parsley leaves,
   finely chopped
1 tomato, deseeded and chopped
1 tablespoon lemon juice
2 tablespoons extra-virgin olive oil
sea salt and freshly ground black pepper

HEMP SEED HUMMUS
120 g hemp seeds*
½ teaspoon finely grated garlic
3 tablespoons olive oil
1 teaspoon ground cumin
a pinch of cayenne pepper, or to taste
2 tablespoons lemon juice, or to taste
2 tablespoons hulled tahini
80 ml (⅓ cup) cold filtered water, plus extra
   if needed

TO SERVE
extra-virgin olive oil
Flatbreads (page 248)
lemon wedges

* See Glossary

Soak eight bamboo skewers in warm water for 20 minutes before using (or use metal skewers).

Place all the tabbouleh ingredients in a bowl and mix well. Stand for 15 minutes to allow the flavours to develop.

Next, place all the hemp seed hummus ingredients in a food processor, add a pinch of salt and blitz until smooth. Add some extra cold filtered water if the hummus is too thick. Set aside.

Place the salmon, melted coconut oil or fat, lemon zest, sumac and cumin in a bowl, and gently toss to coat the salmon. Season with salt and pepper. Thread the salmon onto the skewers, about four pieces per skewer.

Heat a barbecue grill plate to hot or place a chargrill pan over high heat and lightly grease with oil. Add the salmon skewers and cook for 1 minute on each side. Place on a plate and rest for 2 minutes, keeping warm.

Smear the hummus onto a platter, add the tabbouleh and salmon skewers. Drizzle on some olive oil and add a good grind of pepper. Serve with flatbreads and lemon wedges for squeezing over.

JAPANESE CRUMBED BURGER PATTIES

Menchi katsu (or crumbed beef and pork mince patties to you and me) is a popular dish often sold in Japanese butchers and delis. I gotta say, these patties – super juicy inside, super crispy outside – may just become a family favourite. And the sauces we use to accompany them will make you want to go back again and again. A little low-carb salad on the side and some green tea and you are all set for a brilliant weekend meal.

400 ml melted coconut oil

KATSU PATTIES

1 tablespoon coconut oil or good-quality
   animal fat*
1 onion, finely chopped
2 garlic cloves, finely chopped
300 g beef mince
300 g pork mince
2 eggs
½ teaspoon freshly grated nutmeg
sea salt and freshly ground black pepper
150 g (1 ½ cups) almond meal, plus extra if needed
60 g (½ cup) tapioca flour*

TO SERVE

Japanese Mayonnaise (page 251)
Teriyaki Sauce (page 256)
300 g Chinese cabbage (wombok), shredded
200 g daikon, cut into matchsticks
1 carrot, cut into matchsticks
1 spring onion, green part only, cut into matchsticks
1 tablespoon yuzu juice* or lemon juice
2 tablespoons extra-virgin olive oil
1 tablespoon toasted sesame oil
sesame seeds, toasted

* See Glossary

To start on the katsu patties, heat the coconut oil or fat in a frying pan over medium heat. Add the onion and sauté for 5 minutes, or until softened. Add the garlic and cook for 1 minute, or until fragrant. Remove from the heat and allow to cool.

Place the beef and pork mince in a bowl, add the cooled onion mixture, the nutmeg, 1 teaspoon of salt and ½ teaspoon of pepper and mix until combined. Shape into eight even-sized patties.

Place the almond meal in a shallow bowl, season with salt and pepper and mix well. Place the tapioca flour in another shallow bowl. In a third bowl, whisk the eggs with 2 tablespoons of water. Dust the patties with the tapioca flour, shaking off any excess. Working with one patty at a time, dip in the egg mixture, then evenly coat in the seasoned almond meal. Set aside.

Heat the melted coconut oil in a large, deep frying pan over medium–high heat until it reaches 160°C. (To test, place a tiny piece of mince in the oil; if it starts to bubble around the edges immediately, the oil is ready.) Shallow-fry the crumbed patties in batches for 3–5 minutes on both sides until golden and cooked through. Remove from the pan and drain on paper towel. Season with salt and pepper and rest for 5 minutes.

To serve, smear some Japanese mayonnaise on four serving plates, top with two patties, then drizzle over a little teriyaki sauce. Divide the cabbage, daikon, carrot and spring onion among the plates. Combine the yuzu or lemon juice, olive oil and sesame oil in a bowl, season with salt and pepper, then pour over the salad. Finish with a sprinkle of sesame seeds.

CHINESE CUMIN LAMB SKEWERS

These lamb skewers, known as yang rou chuan in China, are next level yum. I have been fascinated by the use of cumin in Chinese dishes ever since I tried some amazing lamb ribs at a Chinese restaurant in Flushing, New York. I have adapted this recipe so it's super quick, yet still delicious, and it's one the whole family will love.

1 kg lamb fillets, cut into 2.5 cm cubes
coconut oil or good-quality animal fat,* for greasing
2 Lebanese cucumbers, deseeded and cut into thin ribbons
1 large handful of coriander leaves
1 spring onion, cut into matchsticks, soaked in ice-cold water for 10 minutes, then drained
sesame seeds, toasted, to serve

CHINESE MARINADE
2 tablespoons cumin seeds
1 tablespoon coriander seeds
2 teaspoons Sichuan pepper
1 tablespoon freshly ground black pepper
2 teaspoons chilli flakes (add more if you like it spicy)
6 garlic cloves, finely chopped
1 teaspoon sea salt
2 tablespoons tamari or coconut aminos*
2 tablespoons lemon juice
3 tablespoons olive oil

DRESSING
2.5 cm piece of ginger, cut into thin matchsticks
1 garlic clove, finely grated
2 tablespoons apple cider vinegar
1 tablespoon toasted sesame oil
3 tablespoons olive oil

* See Glossary

To make the Chinese marinade, combine the cumin, coriander and Sichuan pepper in a frying pan and toast over medium heat for 1 minute until fragrant. Remove from the heat and allow to cool. Stir through the chilli flakes, then use a mortar and pestle to pound the spices until finely ground (or use a spice grinder). Place the ground spices in a large bowl, add the remaining ingredients and mix well.

Add the lamb to the marinade, toss well to coat, then cover and place in the fridge to marinate for 2 hours.

Soak 12 bamboo skewers in warm water for 20 minutes before using (or use metal skewers).

Combine the dressing ingredients in a small bowl. Set aside.

Thread four marinated lamb cubes onto each skewer and set aside on a tray.

Heat a barbecue grill plate to medium–hot or place a large chargrill pan over medium–high heat and grease with a little coconut oil or fat. Cook the lamb for 2–3 minutes on each side, or cook to your liking. Place the skewers on a plate and rest for 5 minutes, keeping warm.

Place the cucumber, coriander and spring onion in a bowl. Add the dressing and gently toss. Season with salt and pepper if needed.

Place the skewers on serving plates, add the salad, then finish with a sprinkle of sesame seeds.

SPICED LAMB, EGGPLANT AND SPINACH GOZLEME

Anyone who loves gozleme will be happy to learn you can easily make a paleo version at home. You could whip this up for a date, an anniversary or any special occasion really. The beauty of gozleme is the way the acid, salt, spice and fat blend harmoniously to take you on a wonderful culinary journey, one bite at a time.

4 eggs
200 g coconut yoghurt
150 g tapioca flour*
sea salt and freshly ground black pepper
2 tablespoons coconut oil or good-quality
    animal fat*
lemon wedges, to serve

LAMB AND SPINACH FILLING

1 large eggplant, cut into 2 cm cubes
200 ml melted coconut oil or good-quality
    animal fat*
3 garlic cloves, finely chopped
2 teaspoons ground cumin
400 g lamb mince
150 g tomato passata
a good pinch of chilli flakes (optional)
2 tablespoons pine nuts, toasted
80 g (1 ¾ cups) baby spinach leaves

* See Glossary

Whisk the eggs, coconut yoghurt and tapioca flour in a large bowl. Season with a pinch of salt and pepper.

Heat 1 teaspoon of the coconut oil or fat in a 20 cm frying pan over medium heat and swirl to coat the base of the pan. Pour in about ½ cup of batter, then tilt and swirl the pan to spread the batter into a thin round. Cook for 1–1 ½ minutes until lightly golden on the underside. Flip and cook on the other side for 30 seconds, or until golden. Set aside. Repeat with the remaining oil or fat and batter to make five or six wraps.

To start on the filling, sprinkle 2 teaspoons of salt over the eggplant and set aside for 1 hour. Rinse and pat dry with paper towel.

In a large, heavy-based saucepan, heat the coconut oil or fat to 160°C over medium heat. (To test, drop a piece of eggplant into the oil; if it starts to bubble around the edges immediately, the oil is ready.) Add the eggplant in batches and fry for 2 minutes, or until golden. Remove with a slotted spoon and drain on paper towel. Set aside. Reserve the oil or fat.

Heat 1 tablespoon of the reserved oil or fat in a frying pan over medium heat. Stir in the garlic and cumin and cook for 20 seconds, or until fragrant. Add the mince, stir with a wooden spoon to break up the lumps, and cook for 8 minutes, or until browned. Reduce the heat to medium–low, add the tomato passata and chilli flakes (if using) and cook, stirring occasionally, for a further 2 minutes until the liquid has almost evaporated. Turn off the heat. Fold through the eggplant, pine nuts and spinach and season with salt and pepper.

Heat a barbecue hotplate and grill plate to medium–hot or place a large frying pan and chargrill pan over medium–high heat. Place ½ cup of lamb mixture on one half of each wrap, then spread out slightly. Fold the wrap over to enclose the filling. Brush one side of each gozleme with the reserved oil or fat and cook on the hotplate or in the pan until the base is golden. Brush the top with more reserved oil or fat, turn and cook until golden.

Meanwhile, chargrill the lemon wedges on the grill plate.

Cut the gozleme into wedges and serve with the lemon wedges.

LAMB KEBABS WITH ZHOUG

The older I get the more I love to cook with skewered meat and seafood, which may have something to do with bringing back great childhood memories. A dish like this is very simple yet looks so impressive. All you need to do is take some lamb, chargrill it and serve it with a really punchy sauce, such as this zhoug.

3 red capsicums
1 kg lamb fillet, cut into 2.5 cm cubes
3 tablespoons coconut oil or good-quality
  animal fat*
2 garlic cloves, finely sliced
3 tablespoons Chicken Bone Broth (page 246)

ZHOUG
45 g (1 ½ cups) coriander leaves
2 large handfuls of flat-leaf parsley leaves
2 jalapeño chillies, deseeded and chopped
  (keep the seeds in if you like it hot)
2 garlic cloves, chopped
3 tablespoons olive oil
¼ teaspoon ground turmeric
1 teaspoon ground cumin
1 teaspoon ground coriander
3 tablespoons apple cider vinegar
sea salt and freshly ground black pepper

* See Glossary

Soak 12 bamboo skewers in warm water for 20 minutes before using (or use metal skewers).

Preheat the oven to 200°C (180°C fan-forced). Lightly grease a baking tray.

Place the whole capsicums on the prepared tray and roast for 15–18 minutes until the skins are blackened and blistered. Immediately place the capsicums in a bowl and cover tightly. (This helps soften the flesh, making them easier to peel.) Set aside for 15 minutes.

Meanwhile, to make the zhoug, place the herbs, chilli and garlic in a food processor and blitz until finely chopped. With the motor running, pour in the olive oil and process until combined, then pour in 3 tablespoons of water and blitz until incorporated. Add the spices and vinegar, season with salt and pepper and process until combined. Set aside.

When the capsicums have cooled, peel off the skin and, using a sharp knife, trim and discard the green stem. Cut in half lengthways, discard the seeds and cut into 3 cm thick strips. Set aside.

Thread three or four lamb cubes onto each skewer and place on a tray. Brush the kebabs with some coconut oil or fat and season with salt and pepper.

Heat a barbecue grill plate to medium–hot or place a chargrill pan over medium–high heat. Grease with a little oil or fat. Cook the kebabs for 2–3 minutes on each side, or cook to your liking. Place on a plate and rest for 5 minutes, keeping warm.

Heat the remaining oil or fat in a frying pan over medium heat. Add the garlic and cook for 1 minute, or until just starting to colour. Add the capsicum, pour in the broth and cook for 2–3 minutes until the capsicum is heated through. Season with salt and pepper.

Tip the capsicum onto a platter, arrange the lamb kebabs on top, then drizzle over the zhoug.

LION'S MANE MUSHROOMS WITH STEAK

SERVES 4

Steak and mushrooms may not be new, but we are discovering many new and amazing properties about mushrooms and the impact they have on our health. Lion's mane mushrooms, which I use in this dish, are believed to support the immune system, help reduce inflammation in the body and benefit the brain, heart and gut. Lion's mane are available from some farmers' markets and specialty grocers, but if you can't find any, oyster, button or portobello mushrooms will also work well.

4 French shallots, quartered lengthways
100 ml melted lard* or good-quality animal fat*
sea salt and freshly ground black pepper
3 tablespoons balsamic vinegar
300 g lion's mane mushrooms, sliced
4 garlic cloves, finely chopped
2 tablespoons chopped flat-leaf parsley leaves
4 x 200–240 g scotch fillet steaks
200 ml Red Wine Jus (page 255)

* See Glossary

Preheat the oven to 180°C (160°C fan-forced).

Place the shallot on a baking tray, drizzle over 1 tablespoon of lard or fat and season with salt and pepper. Roast for 20 minutes, or until cooked through and caramelised. Transfer to a bowl, add the balsamic vinegar and toss to coat. Cover and set aside for 10 minutes to pickle, keeping warm.

Heat 2 tablespoons of the lard or fat in a large, heavy-based frying pan over medium–high heat. Add the mushroom and sauté for 5 minutes, or until starting to colour. Stir in the garlic and parsley and sauté for 1 minute, or until fragrant and the mushroom is cooked through. Season with salt and pepper.

Heat a barbecue hotplate to hot or place a large, heavy-based frying pan over high heat. Coat the steaks with the remaining lard or fat and season with salt and pepper. Sear the steaks on one side for 2 minutes, then flip and cook for another 2–2½ minutes for medium–rare, or cook to your liking. Place the steaks on a plate and rest for 5 minutes, keeping warm.

Heat the jus in a small saucepan over medium–low heat.

Place the steaks on serving plates, add the shallot and mushroom, then pour over the jus and serve.

HANGER STEAK
WITH SALMORIGLIO

SERVES 4

Hanger steak is such a prized cut of beef, butchers have claimed it as their own by calling it butcher's steak. If you are lucky enough to snag one of these incredibly tender steaks, please, don't do too much to it. I like to enhance mine with a herbaceous sauce like this salmoriglio. If you can't find hanger steak, then you can use any other cut you like.

4 x 200 g hanger steaks
3 tablespoons lard* or good-quality animal fat*
freshly ground black pepper

SALMORIGLIO
3 garlic cloves, chopped
sea salt
2 handfuls of oregano leaves
1 handful of flat-leaf parsley leaves
1 long red chilli, deseeded and finely chopped (leave the seeds in if you like it spicy)
100 ml extra-virgin olive oil
juice of 1 lemon

* See Glossary

To make the salmoriglio, pound the garlic and a pinch of salt to a paste using a mortar and pestle (or you can use a hand-held blender or food processor). Add the oregano, parsley and chilli, again pound to a paste, then stir in the olive oil and lemon juice. Season to taste with salt. Set aside.

Heat a barbecue hotplate to hot or place a large, heavy-based frying pan over high heat. Coat the steaks with the lard or fat and season with salt and pepper. Sear the steaks on one side for 3 minutes, then flip and cook for another 3 minutes for medium–rare, or cook to your liking. Place the steaks on a chopping board and rest for 5 minutes, keeping warm.

Slice the steaks and serve with the salmoriglio.

KOREAN BEEF TONGUE

I have to say, Koreans know how to cook beef tongue better than anyone else and, as it's relatively simple to prepare at home, I felt compelled to share this recipe. If you haven't tried tongue, think of it as a very tasty type of steak with an amazing texture. A simple sauce and a side salad or some grilled or steamed veggies are all that's needed to accompany it.

1 x 1.3–1.4 kg beef tongue
1 onion, roughly chopped
1 garlic bulb, halved horizontally
2 celery stalks, roughly chopped
5 fresh bay leaves
sea salt
1 tablespoon black peppercorns

KOREAN SAUCE
1 tablespoon coconut oil or good-quality animal
   fat,* plus extra for brushing
4 garlic cloves, finely chopped
2 long red chillies, deseeded and finely chopped
2 spring onions, white and green parts kept
   separate, both finely chopped
80 ml (⅓ cup) tamari or coconut aminos*
2 tablespoons honey (optional)
1 tablespoon toasted sesame oil
2 tablespoons apple cider vinegar

* See Glossary

Rinse the tongue well under water, then place in a stockpot. Add the onion, garlic, celery, bay leaves, a good pinch of salt and the peppercorns. Cover with water, place over medium heat and bring to the boil. Reduce the heat to low, cover with a lid and gently simmer for 3 hours, or until a knife can be easily inserted into the middle of the flesh with little resistance.

Remove the tongue from the broth and plunge into ice-cold water. Reserve the broth. When cool enough to handle, peel away and discard the skin. Finely slice the tongue and set aside.

Meanwhile, to make the Korean sauce, heat the coconut oil or fat in a saucepan over medium heat. Add the garlic, chilli and white part of the spring onion and sauté for 3–5 minutes until starting to turn golden. Stir in the tamari or coconut aminos, honey (if using), sesame oil, vinegar and 125 ml of reserved broth and bring to the boil. Reduce the heat to low and simmer for 10 minutes, or until the flavours develop.

When ready to serve, heat a chargrill pan over high heat. Brush the tongue slices with the extra coconut oil or fat and season with some salt and pepper. Cook for 15–30 seconds on each side until nice and charred.

Arrange the tongue on a platter, spoon over the Korean sauce, scatter over the green part of the spring onion and serve.

CARNE ASADA WITH FLATBREADS

A huge slab of meat with some guacamole and tomato salsa on the side is just what I crave in summer. I have teamed these with grain-free flatbreads, which can be a little carb heavy when you are on a strict keto regimen, so please feel free to swap them for lettuce or cabbage cups. However, if you like to cycle in and out of ketosis with occasional higher carb days, I encourage you to make some to see how easy and delicious they are.

1 kg flank steak or sirloin steak
2 tablespoons coconut oil or good-quality animal fat*
sea salt and freshly ground black pepper
8 Flatbreads (page 248)
¼ iceberg lettuce, shredded
200 g Keto Sour Cream (page 252)
1 handful of coriander sprigs
lime halves, to serve

MARINADE
80 ml (⅓ cup) olive oil
3 tablespoons tamari or coconut aminos*
1 teaspoon ground cumin
4 garlic cloves, finely grated
3 tablespoons lime juice
2 tablespoons apple cider vinegar
1 tablespoon honey (optional)
1 teaspoon freshly ground black pepper
2 jalapeño chillies, deseeded and finely chopped (leave the seeds in if you like it hot)
3 tablespoons finely chopped coriander leaves

GUACAMOLE
2 avocados, diced
1 tablespoon finely chopped coriander leaves
2 tablespoons lime juice, or to taste
3 tablespoons olive oil

TOMATO SALSA
2 tomatoes, deseeded and cut into 1 cm cubes
¼ red onion, finely chopped
1 tablespoon finely snipped chives
1 tablespoon lime juice
2 tablespoons extra-virgin olive oil

* See Glossary

Combine all the marinade ingredients in a large, shallow bowl.

Add the steak to the marinade and turn to coat. Cover and refrigerate for at least 2 hours or, for best results, overnight. Flip the steak over halfway to evenly marinate.

When ready to cook, heat a barbecue hotplate to medium–hot or place a large, heavy-based frying pan over medium–high heat and brush with the coconut oil or fat.

Season the steak with salt and pepper. Cook the steak on one side, basting with the marinade from time to time, for 6 minutes until charred, then flip and cook for a further 5–6 minutes for medium–rare, or cook to your liking. Place the steak on a plate and rest for 5 minutes, keeping warm.

Place the remaining marinade in a saucepan over medium–low heat. Cook, stirring occasionally, for 3 minutes until heated through.

Place all the guacamole ingredients in a bowl and mix gently. Season with salt and pepper and set aside.

Mix the tomato salsa ingredients in a bowl and season with salt and pepper.

Thickly slice the steak, arrange on a platter and pour over the warm marinade. Serve with the flatbreads, guacamole, tomato salsa, iceberg lettuce, keto sour cream, coriander sprigs and lime halves and let everyone help themselves.

BRAISES AND ONE-POT MEALS

SUMMERY BRAISED FISH WITH OLIVES AND CAPERS

SERVES 4

When summer is in full swing and tomatoes are ripe and bursting with flavour, this is the perfect time to combine some spanking fresh fish with a rustic tomato sauce and the herb that complements tomatoes so well . . . basil. I use fillets here, but you might like to roast or grill a large whole fish, then simply pour the sauce over the top and serve it in the middle of the table. You can, if you like, replace the fish with prawns, crab, mussels, clams or squid; even steak and lamb chops will work extremely well. Serve with any crisp side salad of your choice.

3 tablespoons coconut oil or good-quality
   animal fat*

1 onion, finely chopped

4 garlic cloves, sliced

1 long red chilli, deseeded and sliced

200 g cherry tomatoes, halved

125 g (½ cup) tomato passata

16 pitted kalamata olives, halved

2 tablespoons salted baby capers, rinsed and
   patted dry

375 ml (1 ½ cups) sparkling mineral water

sea salt and freshly ground black pepper

4 x 180 g snapper fillets (or other firm white fish),
   skin on or off, pin-boned

1 large handful of basil leaves, plus extra to serve

lemon wedges, to serve

* See Glossary

Heat 2 tablespoons of the coconut oil or fat in a large frying pan over medium heat. Add the onion and sauté for 5 minutes, or until softened. Add the garlic and chilli and cook for 1 minute, or until fragrant. Stir in the halved tomatoes, passata, olives, capers and mineral water and season with salt and pepper. Bring to the boil, then reduce the heat to low.

Add the fish to the pan and gently cook for 4–6 minutes, flipping halfway through, until just cooked. Transfer the fish to a plate and allow to rest, keeping warm.

Continue to simmer the sauce for 4 minutes, or until reduced and thickened. Stir in the remaining oil or fat and the basil.

Place the fish on warm serving plates, spoon over the sauce and sprinkle on the extra basil leaves. Serve with the lemon wedges on the side.

ROMAN-STYLE CHICKEN

The Italians really know how to make chicken shine without having to work too hard. With the traditional Italian ingredients of tomatoes, garlic, basil and olives, we can create so much flavour that melds perfectly with the chicken and its juices. If you are feeling adventurous, add some chicken livers in the last few minutes of cooking for extra nutritional goodness.

4 large chicken marylands, drumstick and
  thigh separated
sea salt and freshly ground black pepper
3 tablespoons coconut oil or good-quality
  animal fat*
2 onions, chopped
1 red capsicum, deseeded and sliced
1 yellow capsicum, deseeded and sliced
1 celery stalk, chopped
4 garlic cloves, finely chopped
2 tablespoons white wine vinegar
300 g tomato passata
200 ml Chicken Bone Broth (page 246)
250 g cherry tomatoes, halved
2 tablespoons salted baby capers, rinsed and
  patted dry
1 teaspoon dried oregano
2 fresh bay leaves
1 large handful of basil leaves
zucchini noodles, blanched, to serve

* See Glossary

Preheat the oven to 180°C (160°C fan-forced).

Season the chicken pieces with salt and pepper.

Heat 2 tablespoons of the coconut oil or fat in a large, flameproof casserole dish over medium–high heat. Add the chicken pieces in batches and cook on each side for 3–4 minutes until golden. Remove from the dish and set aside.

Reduce the heat to medium and add the remaining oil or fat to the dish. Add the onion and sauté for 3 minutes, or until starting to soften. Stir in the red and yellow capsicum, celery and garlic and sauté for a further 5 minutes, or until softened. Add the vinegar, passata, broth, cherry tomatoes, capers, oregano and bay leaves and bring to a simmer. Season with salt and pepper.

Return the chicken pieces to the dish and stir to coat in the sauce. Transfer to the oven and bake for 45–60 minutes until the chicken is cooked through.

Remove the chicken from the dish and set aside, keeping warm. Place the dish over medium heat and simmer the sauce for about 5–10 minutes until reduced and thickened.

Return the chicken to the dish, scatter over the basil leaves and serve with zucchini noodles.

CHICKEN CACCIATORE

Cacciatore originated in Italy and simply means 'in the style of the hunter'. It's traditionally a braised dish of rabbit or chicken in a rich sauce of tomatoes, garlic and herbs. I adore this dish for so many reasons – it's super simple to make, offers loads of flavour and you can make up a huge batch, so you have some leftover for school or work lunches. It is up to you which cut of chicken you use; I love wings, thighs, marylands and drumsticks. You can also add pan-fried chicken livers, if you want a huge dose of goodness.

3 tablespoons coconut oil or good-quality animal fat*

8 boneless chicken thighs, skin on, chopped into 5 cm pieces

1½ onions, chopped

4 garlic cloves, crushed

2 tablespoons tomato paste

200 ml red wine (such as shiraz)

500 g whole peeled tomatoes, crushed (see Note page 86)

100 ml Chicken Bone Broth (page 246)

2 fresh bay leaves

2 teaspoons finely chopped rosemary

80 g (½ cup) pitted kalamata olives, halved

8 basil leaves, chopped, plus extra to serve

sea salt and freshly ground black pepper

1½ tablespoons apple cider vinegar

1 head of broccoli (about 300 g), cut into florets

1 tablespoon extra-virgin olive oil

720 g (4 cups) cooked Cauliflower Rice (page 246)

* See Glossary

Preheat the oven to 200°C (180°C fan-forced).

Heat the coconut oil or fat in a large, ovenproof frying pan over medium–high heat. Add the chicken in batches and cook for 2 minutes on each side until golden. Remove from the pan and set aside.

Reduce the heat to medium, add the onion and sauté for 5 minutes, or until softened. Stir in the garlic and tomato paste and cook for a further minute. Pour in the wine and simmer for 5 minutes, or until it evaporates. Add the tomatoes, broth, bay leaves, rosemary, olives and chopped basil and season with salt and pepper. Return the chicken to the pan and stir well.

Transfer the pan to the oven and bake for 35 minutes or until the chicken is cooked through. Stir through the vinegar and rest for 5 minutes, keeping warm.

Meanwhile, bring a saucepan of salted water to the boil. Add the broccoli and simmer for 5 minutes, or until tender. Drain well, then tip into a bowl. Drizzle over the olive oil, season with salt and pepper and gently toss.

To serve, spoon the cauliflower rice onto serving plates and top with the chicken cacciatore. Add the broccoli and finish with the extra chopped basil.

STEAMED PORK BELLY WITH MUSHROOMS AND ASIAN GREENS

Asian cultures have an affinity with mushrooms of all types, not only for their culinary uses but also for their health properties, and that is now catching on in other parts of the world. I am a huge fan of mushrooms and I love to incorporate them into my cooking as often as I can. Oyster, shiitake, enoki, lion's mane and so many other varieties with different textures and flavours really enhance a beautiful piece of meat or seafood. Here is a classic pork and mushroom combination.

1 kg boned pork belly, skin scored, at room
    temperature
sea salt
200 ml shaoxing wine or dry sherry
½ teaspoon Chinese five spice
200 g shiitake mushrooms, sliced if large, whole
    if small
100 g oyster mushrooms
freshly ground black pepper
2 spring onions, white part only, cut into matchsticks
1–2 long red chillies, finely sliced

SAUCE
1 tablespoon coconut oil or good-quality
    animal fat*
3 garlic cloves, finely sliced
2.5 cm piece of ginger, cut into matchsticks
2 tablespoons tamari or coconut aminos*
3 tablespoons shaoxing wine or dry sherry
3 tablespoons apple cider vinegar

ASIAN GREENS
1 bunch of Chinese broccoli (gai lan), trimmed and
    halved lengthways
1 bunch of choy sum, trimmed and halved
    lengthways
2 tablespoons extra-virgin olive oil

* See Glossary

Place the pork in a large, non-reactive dish. Rub 1 tablespoon of salt all over the pork, then pour on the shaoxing wine or sherry. Cover and refrigerate for 3 hours to season and tenderise, flipping the pork halfway through.

Wipe the excess salt from the pork and place in a steamer basket over a large saucepan of simmering water. Cover and steam for 2–2 ½ hours until the pork is very tender when pierced with a knife. Place on a plate and rest for 10 minutes, keeping warm.

Meanwhile, to make the sauce, heat the coconut oil or fat in a small saucepan over medium heat. Add the garlic and ginger and cook for 2 minutes, or until softened and fragrant. Add the tamari or coconut aminos, shaoxing wine or sherry and vinegar and bring just to the boil. Reduce the heat to low and gently simmer for 5 minutes to allow the flavours to infuse. Set aside.

Mix the Chinese five spice and 2 teaspoons of salt in a small bowl. Set aside.

Add the shiitake and oyster mushrooms to the steamer, cover and steam for 6 minutes, or until just tender. Transfer to a plate, season with a little five spice salt and pepper and set aside, keeping warm.

Next, for the Asian greens, add the Chinese broccoli and choy sum to the steamer, cover and steam for 5 minutes, or until wilted but still slightly crisp in the centre. Season with a little salt and pepper, drizzle with the olive oil and toss.

Finely slice the pork and arrange on a platter, add the mushrooms and pour over the sauce. Sprinkle the five spice salt over the pork (just enough to your liking), then finish with the spring onion and chilli. Serve with the steamed Asian greens on the side.

DONGPO PORK WITH BOK CHOY

This is one of my favourite Chinese-inspired dishes as it is simply delicious from the first bite to the last. It helps if you are a pork belly fan and a lover of fat (which I am). Dongpo pork is one of the most popular dishes in China for good reason: it is tender, juicy, addictive and melt-in-the-mouth good . . . and if that doesn't sell it to you, then I'm not sure what will. Just make sure you save this for higher carb days when you are cycling out of ketosis.

300 ml shaoxing wine or dry sherry

270 ml tamari or coconut aminos*

250 ml (1 cup) Chicken Bone Broth (page 246)
    or water

230 g honey

1 cinnamon stick

2 star anise

½ teaspoon Chinese five spice

1.2 kg boned pork belly

8 spring onions, halved crossways

5 cm piece of ginger, finely sliced

6 garlic cloves, finely sliced

sea salt and freshly ground black pepper

2 bunches of bok choy, trimmed and halved
    lengthways

1 tablespoon toasted sesame oil

sesame seeds, toasted, to serve

* See Glossary

Place the shaoxing or sherry, tamari or coconut aminos, broth or water, honey, cinnamon stick, star anise and five spice in a large bowl and mix well. Add the pork and toss to coat. Cover and place in the fridge to marinate for at least 2 hours or, for best results, overnight. Flip the pork a few times while marinating to make sure it gets coated evenly.

Preheat the oven to 120°C (100°C fan-forced).

Spread the spring onion halves in an even layer over the base of a roasting tin. (You want them to cover the entire bottom of the tin.) Arrange the ginger and garlic slices evenly on top. Next, place the marinated pork belly, skin-side down, on the bed of spring onion, ginger and garlic. Pour over the marinade.

Cover tightly with foil and bring to a simmer over medium heat. Transfer to the oven and braise, undisturbed, for 1 hour.

Next, flip the pork so it is skin-side up, cover and continue to braise for a further 3 ½–4 hours, or until tender. Transfer the pork to a chopping board and, when cool enough to handle, cut into large chunks.

Increase the oven to 200°C (180°C fan-forced).

Place the tin over medium heat and simmer the sauce for about 15–20 minutes, or until it has reduced enough to coat the back of a spoon. Add the pork pieces and turn to coat in the sauce, then return the tin to the oven and cook for a further 10–15 minutes, turning halfway through.

Just before you are ready to serve, blanch the bok choy in boiling salted water for 2 minutes, or until just cooked through. Drain well, then place in a bowl. Add the sesame oil and toss well. Season with salt and pepper if needed, sprinkle over the sesame seeds and serve with the pork.

RED CHILLI PORK CASSEROLE

SERVES 4-6

Sometimes you need a great hearty dish on a cold winter's night just to feel comforted and nourished, and that is where this no-nonsense pork casserole comes in. It has a bit of spice and is super moreish. I have used pork shoulder, but you can use any stewing or braising cut of pork, chicken or beef here.

1.5 kg boneless pork shoulder, skin removed, cut into 7 cm pieces

sea salt and freshly ground black pepper

3 tablespoons coconut oil or good-quality animal fat*

2 onions, chopped

2 carrots, cut into thick chunks

5 garlic cloves, chopped

2 long red chillies, halved lengthways

1 tablespoon smoked paprika

2 teaspoons caraway seeds

2 tablespoons tomato paste

3 fresh bay leaves

400 g diced tomatoes (see Note page 86)

2 tablespoons apple cider vinegar

250 ml (1 cup) Chicken Bone Broth (page 246)

1 head of broccoli (about 300 g), broken into small florets and stalks cut into 1.5 cm cubes

4 cavolo nero leaves, 3 leaves torn and 1 leaf finely sliced

* See Glossary

Preheat the oven to 150°C (130°C fan-forced).

Season the pork with salt and pepper.

Heat 2 tablespoons of the coconut oil or fat in a flameproof casserole dish over medium–high heat. Add the pork in batches and cook for 5 minutes on all sides until well browned. Remove and set aside.

Reduce the heat to medium, add the remaining oil or fat to the dish, then add the onion and carrot and sauté for 5 minutes, or until the onion is softened. Add the garlic, chilli, paprika and caraway seeds and cook for 1 minute, or until fragrant. Stir in the tomato paste and cook for a further minute.

Return the pork to the dish, add the bay leaves and stir in the tomatoes, vinegar and broth. Bring to the boil, then cover with a lid. Transfer to the oven and bake for 2 hours, or until the meat is almost tender.

Remove from the oven, add the broccoli and cook over low heat for 20 minutes, or until the sauce has reduced slightly and the pork is very tender. Stir in the torn cavolo nero and cook until wilted, about 10 minutes. Taste and season with salt and pepper if needed.

Scatter over the sliced cavolo nero and serve.

IRISH LAMB STEW

As you know, I like to tweak recipes to make them even more nutritious. Here, I use lamb shanks – lamb neck, rump or ribs also work well – and, with apologies to the purists out there, I replace the traditional potato with nutrient-dense sweet potato. I do hope this amazing recipe becomes a family favourite.

2 tablespoons tapioca flour*

sea salt and freshly ground black pepper

4 large lamb shanks

3 tablespoons coconut oil or good-quality animal fat*

1 onion, chopped

½ carrot, chopped

2 celery stalks, chopped

3 French shallots, cut into wedges

2 tablespoons tomato paste

4 garlic cloves, chopped

125 ml (½ cup) red wine (such as shiraz)

1 teaspoon fresh or dried thyme leaves

1 litre (3 cups) Beef or Chicken Bone Broth (page 245 or 246)

2 sweet potatoes (about 500 g), cut into 2 cm cubes

10 Brussels sprouts, halved

chopped flat-leaf parsley leaves, to serve

* See Glossary

Combine the tapioca flour with 1 teaspoon of salt and ½ teaspoon of pepper in a large, shallow bowl. Add the lamb shanks and turn to coat well.

Heat 2 tablespoons of the coconut oil or fat in a large, flameproof casserole dish over medium–high heat. Add the lamb shanks in two batches and sear for 4 minutes on all sides until well browned. Transfer the shanks to a plate and set aside.

Reduce the heat to medium, add the remaining oil or fat, the onion, carrot, celery and shallot and sauté for 7 minutes, or until the veggies start to caramelise. Stir in the tomato paste and cook for 1 minute. Add the garlic and sauté for 30 seconds, or until it is softened and fragrant. Pour in the red wine and stir in the thyme.

Bring to the boil and cook until reduced by half. Stir in the broth, return the shanks to the dish, ensuring the meaty parts are well submerged, and bring to the boil. Reduce the heat to low, cover with a lid and simmer for 2½ hours.

Add the sweet potato and Brussels sprouts to the dish, cover and simmer for a further 30 minutes, or until the meat is tender and falling off the bone.

Carefully remove the whole shanks from the dish and place on a plate. Increase the heat to medium and simmer the stew, uncovered and stirring occasionally to prevent the sauce from catching on the bottom, for 15 minutes, or until thickened.

Return the meat to the dish, stir well, and simmer for 5 minutes, or until the lamb is heated through. Season to taste with salt and pepper.

Ladle the stew into warm bowls, scatter over the parsley and serve.

ITALIAN MEATBALLS

Every home cook needs a staple meatball recipe that they can turn to and tweak until it's perfect. For some, that may mean adding a little more spice, for others it may be a little more pork mince; it could even mean throwing in a little minced chicken liver or bone marrow to make them more nutrient dense. Whatever it is for you, you can't go wrong with this delicious recipe. Serve with some blanched zucchini noodles or steamed greens.

400 g pork mince

200 g beef mince

6 Garlic Confit cloves (page 250) or 3 raw garlic cloves, crushed

1 teaspoon chilli flakes (optional)

1 teaspoon fennel seeds, toasted and coarsely ground

2 tablespoons finely chopped flat-leaf parsley leaves

1¼ teaspoons sea salt

½ teaspoon freshly ground black pepper

3 tablespoons good-quality animal fat*

TOMATO AND BASIL SAUCE

2 tablespoons good-quality animal fat*

1 large onion, chopped

4 garlic cloves, finely sliced

600 g whole peeled tomatoes, crushed (see Note page 86)

250 ml (1 cup) Chicken Bone Broth (page 246)

1 handful of basil leaves, plus extra to serve

* See Glossary

Place the pork and beef mince, garlic, chilli flakes (if using), fennel seeds, parsley, salt and pepper in a bowl and mix well. Shape the mixture into 20 walnut-sized balls. Place on a tray, cover and refrigerate until needed.

To make the tomato and basil sauce, heat the fat in a large saucepan over medium–low heat. Add the onion and sauté for 5 minutes, or until softened. Add the garlic and cook for a further 30 seconds, or until fragrant. Stir in the tomatoes and broth and bring to the boil. Reduce the heat to low and simmer, stirring occasionally, for 30 minutes, or until thickened. Add the basil and simmer for a further 5 minutes. Blend the sauce with a hand-held blender until smooth. Season to taste with salt and pepper.

Heat the fat in a large, heavy-based frying pan over medium–high heat. Add the meatballs, in batches if necessary, and fry, shaking the pan occasionally, for 5 minutes, or until golden. Pour in the tomato and basil sauce, reduce the heat to medium and bring to a simmer. Cook for a further 5 minutes, or until the meatballs are just cooked through. Season to taste.

Sprinkle over the extra basil and finish with a good grind of pepper.

VEGGIE SIDES

CROATIAN CUCUMBER SALAD

When I was a young chef, I tried to show off by seeing how many flavours and ingredients I could put on one plate with the belief that more is more. Over time my perception has shifted a great deal – in fact, the older I get, the simpler I like to make my life. These days it is about focusing on just a few ingredients and making them shine. This Croatian cucumber salad is the perfect example of how delicious a few well-chosen ingredients can be.

4 Lebanese cucumbers (about 400 g in total), finely sliced into ribbons or rounds (or a combination of both)
2 garlic cloves, finely grated
2 tablespoons white wine vinegar or apple cider vinegar
sea salt and freshly ground black pepper
½–1 teaspoon chilli flakes (optional)
2 tablespoons extra-virgin olive oil
2–3 sprigs of dill, roughly torn

Place all the ingredients in a bowl, add 1 tablespoon of water and toss to combine. Taste and season with more salt and pepper if needed.

Refrigerate for about 30 minutes or until chilled, then serve.

CELERY SALAD WITH ALMONDS

Have you ever bought a bunch of celery and not known what to do with the leftovers after making a broth or juice? Celery actually makes for a delicious salad with just a few complementary ingredients – fresh herbs, a flavourful dressing and crunchy toasted nuts to add some texture. This may well become one of your go-to salads, as it is cheap and the whole family will love it (just keep the chilli on the side if your kids don't like spice).

4 celery stalks, finely sliced
   diagonally
2 handfuls of coriander leaves
2 spring onions, green part only,
   sliced diagonally
1 long red chilli, sliced diagonally
70 g almonds (activated if possible),*
   toasted and chopped

DRESSING
2 tablespoons lemon juice
100 ml extra-virgin olive oil
½ teaspoon finely grated garlic
sea salt and freshly ground black
   pepper

* See Glossary

Place all the dressing ingredients in a bowl and whisk well. Taste and season with more salt and pepper if needed.

Place the celery, coriander, spring onion, chilli and almonds in a bowl. Pour over the dressing and gently toss the salad until evenly coated. Arrange in a bowl or on a platter and serve.

ITALIAN CHOPPED SALAD

When I was at school I had some friends who were from Italian families and their lunchboxes were always fascinating to me. They had ingredients like olives, salami, mortadella, cheese, greens and capsicums, and were so different from mine and many others at our school. This did not seem to bother them and I was always in awe of how much they loved their food. This memory has stayed with me and is a reminder that it is always okay to be yourself, even if it means going against the grain. Here is my version of the classic Italian chopped salad – I wish I could have had this in my lunchbox!

200 g marinated artichokes, drained and chopped

2 baby cos lettuces, trimmed and leaves roughly chopped

18 pitted kalamata olives, halved

150 g sliced mortadella

12 semi-dried tomatoes, chopped

1 handful of flat-leaf parsley leaves, roughly chopped

1 handful of basil leaves, torn

100 g dairy-free feta, chopped (optional)

1 tablespoon hemp seeds*

ITALIAN DRESSING

2 tablespoons white wine vinegar

1 teaspoon Dijon mustard

1 garlic clove, finely grated

½ teaspoon dried Italian seasoning

3 tablespoons extra-virgin olive oil

sea salt and freshly ground black pepper

* See Glossary

Place all the Italian dressing ingredients in a bowl and whisk to combine. Taste and season with more salt and pepper if needed.

Place the artichoke, lettuce, olives, mortadella, semi-dried tomato, herbs and feta (if using) in a large bowl, add the dressing and gently toss. Sprinkle with hemp seeds and some more pepper and serve.

PERSIAN SALAD WITH ZA'ATAR VINAIGRETTE

Middle Eastern food never fails to entice me with its use of herbs and spices, and I am growing to love this cuisine more and more each time I try a new recipe. This is a great example of a side dish that can be just as exciting as a main. This salad would go beautifully with a platter of juicy prawns that have been chargrilled with sumac and garlic, a braised dish of spiced lamb or grilled salmon that has been cooked to medium–rare then flaked through the salad. Your imagination is all you need so please don't be afraid to experiment!

3 Lebanese cucumbers, cut into 2 cm cubes

1 yellow capsicum, deseeded and cut into
   2 cm cubes

5 radishes, cut into 1 cm thick wedges

½ red onion, finely diced

1 handful of dill fronds

1 handful of mint leaves

1 handful of flat-leaf parsley leaves

100 g pistachio nuts (activated if possible),*
   toasted and roughly chopped

ZA'ATAR VINAIGRETTE

1 garlic clove, finely grated

80 ml (⅓ cup) extra-virgin olive oil

3 tablespoons red wine vinegar

2 teaspoons za'atar*

sea salt and freshly ground black pepper

* See Glossary

Place all the za'atar vinaigrette ingredients in a bowl and whisk well. Taste and season with more salt and pepper if needed.

Place the cucumber, capsicum, radish, onion, herbs and pistachios in a large bowl. Pour over the vinaigrette and gently toss to combine. Transfer the salad to a platter and serve.

INDIAN-SPICED CRISPY OKRA SALAD

If you have read my other cookbooks, you will know I have a bit of a thing for okra. I am not going to lie – it may just be one of my all-time favourite greens. This Indian okra salad would be lovely alongside some spiced lamb chops, wild salmon or even a delicious curry. If okra isn't your thing, you can simply swap it for sliced zucchini, broccoli or cauliflower florets, snow peas, green beans or asparagus and the recipe will still be absolutely delicious.

1 teaspoon cumin seeds

1 teaspoon ground coriander

1½ teaspoons ground turmeric

2 teaspoons garam masala

coconut oil or good-quality animal fat,*
　　for shallow-frying

600 g fresh okra pods, trimmed and cut
　　into long strips

sea salt

1 small red onion, finely chopped

4 tomatoes, deseeded and cut into strips

1 large handful of coriander leaves, roughly
　　chopped

1 tablespoon lemon juice

chilli flakes, to taste (optional)

* See Glossary

Toast the cumin seeds in a frying pan over medium heat for 20 seconds, or until fragrant.

Combine the cumin seeds with all the other spices in a small bowl and set aside.

In a large, heavy-based saucepan, heat 3 cm of coconut oil or fat to 180°C over medium–high heat. (To test, drop a small piece of okra into the oil – it should bubble instantly around the edges.) Add the okra in batches and fry, stirring occasionally, for 3 minutes, or until golden and crispy. Remove with a slotted spoon and drain on paper towel. Season generously with salt and a couple of pinches of the spice mix.

Place the okra, red onion, tomato, coriander and lemon juice in a large bowl and gently toss. Season the salad with more salt if needed, sprinkle over the remaining spice mix and the chilli flakes (if using) and serve.

ASIAN GREENS WITH COCONUT AND LIME SAUCE

SERVES 4

The combination of Asian greens and coconut may seem a little unusual, but I encourage you to give this a whirl as it is a beautiful side dish to so many different Asian-inspired mains. The lime helps to bring acidity, which perfectly balances the richness of the coconut and gives the greens some zing too.

2 bunches of choy sum (about 350 g), trimmed

2 bunches of bok choy (about 240 g), trimmed

2 spring onions, trimmed

400 ml coconut milk

5 cm piece of ginger, cut into fine matchsticks

1 lemongrass stem, pale part only, bruised and halved

1 tablespoon fish sauce, plus extra if needed

1 tablespoon lime juice

sea salt (optional)

1 teaspoon toasted sesame oil

Fermented Chilli Sambal (page 248), to serve (optional)

lime cheeks, to serve

Cut the choy sum, bok choy and spring onions into 8 cm lengths. Keep the stems and leaves of the choy sum and bok choy separate and the green and white parts of the spring onion separate. Set aside.

Pour the coconut milk into a large saucepan, add the ginger and lemongrass and place over medium heat. Bring to the boil, then reduce the heat to low and simmer for 5 minutes, or until fragrant. Add the white part of the spring onion and the choy sum and bok choy stems, cover and simmer for 2 minutes, or until almost tender.

Add the green part of the spring onion and the leaves of the choy sum and bok choy to the pan, cover and simmer for a further 2 minutes, or until the vegetables are tender. Gently stir through the fish sauce and lime juice. Taste and add more fish sauce or season with salt if desired.

Arrange the veggies in a serving bowl, ladle over the coconut and lime sauce and drizzle over the sesame oil. Serve with the fermented chilli sambal (if using) and lime cheeks on the side.

ROAST VEG WITH NUTRITIONAL YEAST

Nutritional yeast is an ingredient that is grown on a mixture of cane and beet molasses. It is available from health food stores and is rich in fibre, protein, B vitamins and zinc. The yeast has a delicious cheesy, nutty flavour and can be used in many different ways – add it to pesto and salad dressings, stir it through soups for a flavour boost, or sprinkle it over roast veggies like I have done here.

1 onion, sliced

1 head of broccoli (about 300 g), stalk and florets thickly cut into 6–8 pieces

2 zucchini, thickly sliced diagonally

300 g savoy cabbage, cut into wedges

3 baby golden beetroot, halved lengthways

1 garlic bulb, cloves separated

3 tablespoons coconut oil or good-quality animal fat*

sea salt and freshly ground black pepper

125 ml (½ cup) Chicken Bone Broth (page 246)

½ bunch cavolo nero (about 150 g), stems discarded and leaves torn (use the stems for broths or soups)

1 tablespoon chopped rosemary leaves

2 tablespoons nutritional yeast*

* See Glossary

Preheat the oven to 200°C (180°C fan-forced). Line a large roasting tin with baking paper.

Combine the onion, broccoli, zucchini, cabbage, beetroot and garlic in the prepared tin, toss with the coconut oil or fat and season with salt and pepper.

Spread out the vegetables in a single layer, making sure they're not too bunched up. Pour in the broth and roast for 20 minutes. Add the cavolo nero and rosemary and roast for a further 20 minutes, or until the vegetables are tender and golden.

Arrange the roast vegetables on a platter, sprinkle over the nutritional yeast and serve.

DR PETE'S COLD AND FLU TONIC

Dr Peter Bablis – chiropractor, acupuncturist, herbalist and homeopath with a PhD for his clinical work on Neuro-Emotional Technique (NET) – has helped me and many others on their health journey. One of the best pieces of advice I got from my dear friend and mentor when I entered his clinic 25 years ago was to make up his cold and flu tonic recipe. It is advice I too have shared over time, and now I get to share it with you in the hope that you will, in turn, pass it on to your loved ones.

4 garlic bulbs
5 cm piece of ginger
3 lemons
manuka honey, to taste (optional)

Roughly chop the garlic, ginger and lemons, place in a large saucepan and cover with 2 litres of water. Bring to the boil, then reduce the heat to low and simmer for 1 hour.

Strain the tonic into a jug, add the manuka honey to taste and drink up to four glasses per day. Store in an airtight glass bottle in the fridge for up to 1 week.

TURMERIC AND GINGER ELIXIR

Dr John Teh from PlantMed in Brisbane is one of the most beautiful human beings I've had the pleasure of knowing. John makes a remarkable beverage called Dr Teh's Turmeric Elixir and our freezer is always stocked with bottles of it. When we harvest turmeric from our garden, we also like to make our own elixir. I encourage you to look at the work Dr Teh is doing, as he presents a very compelling approach to using nature, alongside modern medicine, as a tool for health. This recipe is inspired by Dr Teh's elixir.

500 g fresh turmeric

300 g ginger

2 ½ tablespoons filtered water

2 teaspoons monk fruit sweetener*
    or manuka honey, or to taste

¼ teaspoon ground cinnamon

a pinch of freshly ground black
    pepper

* See Glossary

You'll need a 500 ml preserving jar with a lid for this recipe. Wash the jar in very hot water or run it through a hot rinse cycle in the dishwasher.

Juice the turmeric and ginger in a cold press juicer. Mix in the water, sweetener, cinnamon and pepper and pour into the sterilised jar. Cover and allow to steep for 1 hour before drinking.

Take as a 25 ml dose up to three times a day. Store the turmeric elixir in the fridge for up to 5 days.

CHAI-SPICED ROOIBOS TEA

Anyone who knows me will tell you I usually travel with a drink bottle of hot herbal tea. I love to mix things up and go through many different types of tea. One day rooibos, the next chamomile, then peppermint or pure green, licorice, ginger, lemongrass . . . you get the picture! Tea is also the drink I enjoy in the morning when I'm fasting. I recommend anyone who's a coffee drinker swap over to this chai-spiced rooibos tea or other herbal teas for a month or two and see how you feel.

375 ml (1 ½ cups) plant-based milk of your choice
   (such as almond or coconut)
1 teaspoon finely grated ginger
sweetener of your choice (liquid stevia,* xylitol,*
   monk fruit sweetener,* honey), to taste

CHAI-SPICED ROOIBOS TEA
2 cinnamon sticks
1 ½ teaspoons cardamom pods
1 teaspoon cloves
40 g (¾ cup) loose rooibos tea leaves
1 teaspoon black peppercorns
1 teaspoon Chinese five spice

* See Glossary

To make the chai-spiced rooibos tea, break the cinnamon sticks into small shards and place in a mortar. Add the cardamom pods and cloves and pound with a pestle until coarsely ground (or use a spice grinder). Transfer to a bowl, add the rooibos tea leaves, peppercorns and five spice and mix well.

Pour the milk into a small saucepan and mix in the ginger and 3 teaspoons of chai-spiced rooibos tea. Cover with a lid and warm over medium–low heat for 5 minutes. Don't let the milk boil.

Remove the pan from the heat and let steep, covered, for about 10 minutes to allow the flavours to infuse. If needed, reheat to the desired temperature – again, don't allow the milk to boil.

Strain the tea into a mug or glass, sweeten with your sweetener of choice and enjoy!

Transfer the remaining chai-spiced rooibos tea to an airtight container and store in the pantry for up to 3 months.

HEMP KOMBUCHA WITH SCHISANDRA BERRIES

MAKES 2.5 LITRES

Adding hemp oil to kombucha is a great way to get some extra healthy fat into your body on a daily basis. Kombucha is delicious and high in probiotics, and if you haven't made it at home, I encourage you to give it a crack. Schisandra berries are very potent and pack a punch, so go easy. You can usually pick some up online or at health food stores. Scoby stands for 'symbiotic culture of bacteria and yeast', and the scoby is essential for creating this fermented drink. If you don't have a friend who can gift you one, you can find starter kits to make your own at health food stores or online.

2.75 litres filtered water, plus extra if needed

200 g raw sugar

25 g (⅓ cup) loose black tea leaves

125 ml (½ cup) pre-made kombucha (from a previous batch or a store-bought bottle)

1 scoby

1–2 tablespoons schisandra berry powder or berries

½–1 teaspoon hemp oil,* per serve

* See Glossary

You will need a 4 litre glass jar and four 750 ml glass bottles with screw-top lids for this recipe. To sterilise the jars, wash them in very hot, soapy water and run them through a hot rinse cycle in your dishwasher.

Bring 750 ml of the filtered water to the boil in a stainless steel saucepan. Add the raw sugar and stir until dissolved. Remove from the heat and add the tea leaves. Set aside to cool for 1–3 hours.

Strain the sweet tea through a fine strainer into the sterilised 4 litre jar and add the kombucha and scoby. Fill the jar with the remaining filtered water to 5 cm from the top, adding extra if needed. Cover the top of the jar with a double layer of muslin (dipped in apple cider vinegar) and secure with a rubber band. Leave the jar in a warm, dark, well-ventilated place with a temperature of 18–28°C.

After 8–12 days of fermenting, taste your kombucha. It should be slightly sweet and sour, with just a hint of tea. If it's too sweet, leave it to ferment for a few more days. If you're happy with it, use clean hands to remove the scoby and separate it from the new one. You now have two scobies, which you can use to make more kombucha (or gift one of them to a friend). If you don't wish to make another batch straight away, store the scobies in a solution of sweetened tea on the bench. Don't put them in the fridge or they will go into hibernation.

Mix the schisandra berry powder or berries into the kombucha and transfer to the sterilised glass bottles, leaving about 2.5 cm free at the top. Leave at room temperature on the kitchen bench for 3–5 days (depending on your taste) before refrigerating.

When ready to drink, pour the kombucha into a tall glass and add the hemp oil to taste.

BULLETPROOF COFFEE OR TEA

Adding some fat to your coffee or tea is a great way to stay in ketosis. You may have heard of bulletproof coffee, made famous by Dave Asprey, the father of biohacking. Well, before that, Paul Chek, a friend of mine, added yak's or cow's butter to his coffee – a trick he learnt from the Tibetans. As I don't consume dairy, I use coconut cream and MCT oil instead. Give this a try in your next brew and see how you feel. Oh, by the way, too much MCT oil can make you go to the bathroom, so go easy!

200 ml hot black coffee, strong black
    tea or herbal tea of your choice
2 ½ tablespoons coconut cream or
    plant-based milk of your choice
1 tablespoon coconut oil
1 tablespoon MCT oil* (see Note)
sweetener of your choice (liquid
    stevia,* xylitol,* monk fruit
    sweetener,* honey), to taste
    (optional)
ground cinnamon, to serve

* See Glossary

Place the coffee or tea, coconut cream or milk, coconut oil, MCT oil and sweetener (if using) in a blender and whiz for 10 seconds, or until pale in colour.

Pour into a coffee cup or latte glass, sprinkle a little cinnamon over the top and serve.

NOTE If you'd prefer not to use MCT oil, simply replace it with more coconut oil.

GINGER SWITCHEL

If you haven't heard of switchel before, it's one of the world's first soft drinks, made from adding apple cider vinegar, spices and herbs to still or sparking water or coconut water. It is a great alternative to kombucha or kefir as the apple cider vinegar is wonderful on the gut and has anti-inflammatory properties.

1 litre coconut water
2 tablespoons apple cider vinegar
1–2 tablespoons monk fruit
    sweetener,* maple syrup or honey
1 tablespoon finely chopped ginger
ice cubes, to serve

* See Glossary

You'll need a 1.5 litre preserving jar with a lid for this recipe. Wash the jar in very hot water or run it through a hot rinse cycle in the dishwasher.

Place the coconut water, vinegar, sweetener and ginger in the prepared jar and mix well. Cover and refrigerate for 12 hours to infuse.

After 12 hours, strain the ginger switchel into glasses, add some ice and serve.

CHOCOLATE SMOOTHIE WITH HEMP AND WATTLESEED

Is it a drink, a breakfast, a snack or a dessert? I'll leave that up to you to answer! The one thing I can say about this recipe is it's absolutely delicious. Wattleseed is a native Australian ingredient that tastes a bit like a combination of coffee and cacao. Don't worry if you don't have this ingredient though – your smoothie will still taste sensational without it. Having said that, I encourage you to go online and look up Australian native herbs and spices. Order a small amount to start with and begin to include some in your diet. Australian native ingredients are some of the most nutrient-packed foods on the planet.

3 tablespoons cacao powder

1 avocado, roughly chopped and frozen

2 tablespoons almond butter

1 vanilla pod, split and seeds scraped

500 ml (2 cups) Hemp Milk (page 250) or almond milk

sweetener of your choice (liquid stevia,* xylitol,* monk fruit sweetener,* honey), to taste

TO SERVE

sliced strawberries

shaved chocolate

hemp seeds*

ground wattleseed

cacao nibs

macadamia nuts (activated if possible),* toasted and roughly chopped

* See Glossary

Place the cacao powder, avocado, almond butter, vanilla, hemp or almond milk and sweetener in a high-speed blender and whiz until smooth.

Pour the smoothie into serving bowls or glasses. Arrange the strawberries and shaved chocolate on top, then sprinkle over the hemp seeds, wattleseed, cacao nibs and macadamias.

HEMP AND CHARCOAL SMOOTHIE

Charcoal has been used for many years to help rid the body of toxins. I use it from time to time, especially after flying, and add it to lots of different things, such as kombucha, kefir, filtered water, coconut yoghurt, smoothies and keto breads and spreads.

150 g frozen blueberries

1 handful of baby spinach leaves

8 mint leaves

15 macadamia or cashew nuts (activated if possible),* soaked in water for 2 hours

2 teaspoons activated charcoal*

500 ml (2 cups) Hemp Milk (page 250), plus extra to reach desired consistency

½ teaspoon diatomaceous earth* (optional)

35 g (¼ cup) ice cubes

manuka honey or sweetener of your choice (liquid stevia,* xylitol,* monk fruit sweetener*), to taste (optional)

TO SERVE

fresh or frozen blueberries

fresh or frozen raspberries

hemp seeds*

* See Glossary

Place the blueberries, spinach, mint, macadamias or cashews, activated charcoal, hemp milk, diatomaceous earth (if using) and ice in a high-speed blender and whiz until smooth.

Add some manuka honey or sweetener and more hemp milk, if desired. Whiz again, pour into glasses or bowls, scatter over the berries and hemp seeds and serve immediately.

JAFFA TRUFFLES

As a kid growing up in the 1970s and 1980s the famous Jaffa lollies left a lasting impression on me. Funnily enough, I was never a fan of how hard they were on the outside, so I have reinterpreted them into a luxurious truffle with that hint of orange that works so well. Now, I know some people really dislike chocolate and orange together, so feel free to swap the orange for coffee, strawberry, mint, salt or whatever flavouring puts a smile on your dial.

300 g coconut oil or ghee*

200 g coconut butter

2 tablespoons coconut cream

3 tablespoons manuka honey (or liquid stevia*, to taste)

600 g dark (70–90% cacao) chocolate, chopped

4–5 drops of essential orange oil

cacao powder, for dusting

* See Glossary

You'll need to start these a day ahead.

Line a large tray with baking paper.

Place the coconut oil or ghee, coconut butter, coconut cream and honey in the bowl of an electric mixer fitted with the paddle attachment. Mix, scraping down the side of the bowl from time to time, until pale and creamy.

Meanwhile, melt half the chocolate in a heatproof bowl over a saucepan of just-simmering water. (Make sure the bowl doesn't touch the water or it will overheat and the chocolate will seize.) Stir in the orange oil with a metal spoon. Leave to cool until still runny but not hot.

With the motor still running, slowly pour the melted chocolate into the coconut oil or ghee mixture and mix until combined and a little fluffy. (If it becomes soft and runny, simply pop it in the fridge for 30–50 minutes, or until cool and slightly firm, then mix again using the electric mixer until whipped and fluffy.)

Spoon the chocolate mixture into a piping bag fitted with an 8 mm straight-edge nozzle. Pipe 1 cm chocolate teardrop shapes onto the prepared tray, then place in the fridge for 1 hour, or until firm.

Melt the remaining chocolate, then cool slightly. Using a fork, dip the chocolate teardrops into the melted chocolate, gently shake to remove the excess, return to the tray and dust in the cacao powder. Refrigerate, uncovered, overnight to set.

Place the jaffa truffles on a platter and serve. Store the truffles in an airtight container in the fridge for up to 3 weeks.

CHOCOLATE MUD CAKE

SERVE 6-8

Sometimes you have to bring out the big guns and go all out. When you have a party or event – whether it be a farewell, anniversary, birthday or school fete – and you really want to impress, then this chocolate mud cake is the answer. It is low in carbs but super rich, decadent and, most importantly, delicious.

300 g dark (85–90% cacao) chocolate, chopped
200 ml melted coconut oil or ghee*
6 eggs, separated
180 g finely ground monk fruit sweetener*
150 g (1½ cups) almond meal
2 teaspoons baking powder
a pinch of sea salt
100 g raspberries
Raspberry and Chia Sauce (page 239), to serve

CHOCOLATE GANACHE
120 g dark (85–90% cacao) chocolate, finely
  chopped
150 ml coconut cream, plus extra if needed

* See Glossary

Preheat the oven to 160°C (140°C fan-forced). Grease a 25 cm round cake tin and line the base and side with baking paper.

Combine the chocolate and coconut oil or ghee in a heatproof bowl and place over a saucepan of just-simmering water. Stir occasionally with a metal spoon until melted and smooth. (Make sure the bowl doesn't touch the water or it will overheat and the chocolate will seize.)

Meanwhile, place the egg yolks and half the monk fruit sweetener in the bowl of an electric mixer and mix on medium–high speed using the whisk attachment until the mixture is doubled in size and fluffy. Fold into the melted chocolate mixture until incorporated. Sift in the almond meal, baking powder and salt and fold through.

Clean the bowl and whisk attachment. Add the egg whites and the remaining monk fruit sweetener to the bowl and whisk until soft peaks form.

Gently fold the egg white mixture into the chocolate mixture. Pour into the prepared tin and smooth the top with a spatula. Bake for 40 minutes, or until the cake has risen a little and is cooked through. (The cake is cooked when a skewer inserted in the centre comes out clean.) Allow to cool completely in the tin, then place in the refrigerator for 4 hours to chill.

To make the chocolate ganache, place the chocolate in a heatproof bowl and set aside. Pour the coconut cream into a small saucepan and bring to the boil over low heat. Remove from the heat and slowly pour over the chocolate, stirring constantly with a metal spoon, until the chocolate has melted and the ganache is smooth and shiny. If the ganache looks like it is splitting, add a dash of extra coconut cream and mix to incorporate.

Turn the chilled cake out onto a platter and spread the chocolate ganache over the top. Scatter over the raspberries and drizzle over the raspberry and chia sauce.

AVOCADO AND MINT ICE CREAM

SERVES 4

When summer is in full force and avocados are plentiful, delicious and at their cheapest, I buy a lot and make this wonderful non-dairy ice cream. Avocado is the main ingredient and the mint adds a cooling freshness and bright note to this treat. If you want to take your ice cream to another level, simply drizzle some good-quality melted chocolate over the top to create your own ice-cream magic. Mmmm . . . just like the old days.

2 avocados, halved, flesh scooped
   out and frozen
350 ml coconut cream
4–6 drops of essential peppermint
   oil, or to taste
¼ teaspoon liquid stevia*
mint leaves, to serve

* See Glossary

Combine the avocado, coconut cream, peppermint oil and liquid stevia in a high-speed blender and whiz until smooth.

Pour the mixture into an airtight container, cover and freeze for 2 hours.

Scoop the ice cream into bowls, scatter on the mint and serve.

RASPBERRY AND AVOCADO ICE CREAM

Growing up on Queensland's Gold Coast, where the weather was generally warm all year round, ice cream was my go-to treat. However, it took me some time to work out that dairy was not my friend. At the age of 19 I took it out of my diet and my health improved in a huge way, but the dilemma was I still wanted to eat ice cream. So, over the next few decades, I came up with some amazing dairy-free versions that are, in my opinion, just as good, if not better! You will love this raspberry and avocado number.

600 g frozen raspberries
2 avocados, halved and flesh
    scooped out
2 teaspoons lemon juice
½ teaspoon finely grated lemon zest
1 vanilla pod, split and seeds scraped
3 tablespoons finely ground monk
    fruit sweetener* or xylitol,*
    or to taste

* See Glossary

Place all the ingredients in a high-speed blender and whiz until smooth. If you like your ice cream a little sweeter, taste and add more sweetener, then blend to combine.

You can eat this straight away while it is still nice and creamy or, if it's too soft, transfer to an airtight container and freeze for 1 hour to firm up.

CHOCOLATE-DIPPED SHORTBREAD

A good biscuit is something that will always be appreciated by this chef. My wife Nic actually created a nut- and grain-free cookie named after my daughters so the girls could take them to school – we call them 'chiindi cookies'. Aside from those, shortbread is one of life's simple joys, so I developed this keto version for you to enjoy with tea, while staying healthy. You don't need to dip them in chocolate if you don't wish to, but for me that is the crowning glory.

240 g coconut oil or ghee*

160 g almond meal

160 g tapioca flour*

110 g finely ground monk fruit sweetener* or xylitol,*
    plus extra for dusting

a pinch of sea salt

100 g dark (80–90% cacao) chocolate, chopped

* See Glossary

Preheat the oven to 150°C (130°C fan-forced). Grease a baking tray and line with baking paper.

Combine the coconut oil or ghee, almond meal and tapioca flour in a bowl and rub the oil or ghee into the dry ingredients with your fingertips. Add the sweetener and salt and mix well.

Transfer the shortbread mixture to the prepared tray and spread it out evenly to form a 35 cm x 23 cm rectangle. Pat down to flatten to an 8 mm thickness and dock with a fork.

Bake for 30 minutes, or until pale golden. Remove from the oven and, while still hot, cut the shortbread with the tip of a knife into 8 cm x 4 cm rectangles. Allow to cool, then place in the fridge to chill for 1 hour.

Meanwhile, melt the chocolate in a heatproof bowl over a saucepan of just-simmering water. (Make sure the bowl doesn't touch the water or it will overheat and the chocolate will seize.)

Use a pastry brush to brush half of each shortbread piece with the melted chocolate. Place back on the tray and return to the fridge for 15 minutes to set. Dust with a little extra sweetener and serve.

MIXED BERRY JELLY CUPS

Jelly cups are super easy to make – they only take a few minutes of preparation and a little time to set in the fridge. What I love about jelly cups is you are getting a great dose of good-quality gelatine into your system while enjoying a delicious treat. You can flavour them with whatever fruit is in season. If you are following a strict keto approach, then berries, especially wild berries, or Australian native fruit are perfect as they are relatively low carb. If you can get your hands on some, try Davidson plums or quandongs. You can also top your jelly cups with whipped coconut cream if you want to make them even more special.

1 tablespoon powdered gelatine*

500 ml (2 cups) coconut water

100 g frozen mixed berries (raspberries, blueberries, strawberries, blackberries)

sweetener of your choice (liquid stevia,* xylitol,* monk fruit sweetener,* honey), to taste (optional)

200 g fresh mixed berries (raspberries, blueberries, strawberries, blackberries)

mint leaves, to serve

* See Glossary

Place 3 tablespoons of water in a small bowl and sprinkle over the gelatine. Set aside to soak for 2 minutes.

Combine the coconut water, frozen mixed berries and sweetener (if using) in a small saucepan over medium heat and stir well. Bring to a simmer, then reduce the heat to low and simmer for 10 minutes.

Add the gelatine mixture to the hot berry liquid and stir until the gelatine has dissolved. Strain through a fine strainer into a jug; discard the mixed berry pulp.

Pour the jelly mixture into six small glasses or ramekins, add half the fresh berries and chill in the fridge for 4 hours, or until set. To serve, scatter over the remaining berries and some mint leaves.

NIC'S CAMU CAMU SLAB

Making homemade chocolate would have to be one of life's simplest pleasures. You will wonder why you ever spent so much money buying chocolate when you can make it so easily at home. My wife, Nic, makes a slab like this every week or two to have on hand as a treat and we often send guests home with a small goody bag of a few pieces. This recipe features camu camu berry powder, which adds a hit of vitamin C and a lovely tang to the chocolate.

100 ml melted coconut oil

100 g cacao butter, melted

3 tablespoons cacao powder

3 tablespoons carob powder

1 teaspoon camu camu berry powder

80 g honey

1 teaspoon ground cinnamon

250 g macadamia nuts (activated if possible),* toasted and roughly chopped

a pinch of sea salt

* See Glossary

Line a 26 cm x 16 cm tray with plastic wrap.

Place all the ingredients in a bowl and stir well. Spread out on the prepared tray and place in the fridge for 2 hours, or until set. (If you are in a hurry, pop the slab in the freezer and it will set even faster.)

Turn out the slab onto a chopping board and chop or break into bite-sized pieces.

You will need to store the chocolate in an airtight container in the fridge, as they will melt at room temperature. They will keep for 2–3 weeks, but if your family is like mine, they won't last nearly that long.

TURKISH DELIGHT

If you have never tried rosewater, it is very difficult to describe but is a flavour you will never forget as it's so distinctive. My first mouthful of Turkish delight was a revelation and from that day on I have been a huge fan of this treat. The great news is that it's very simple to make a keto version at home. I encourage you to try this recipe in all its fragrant glory.

50 g powdered gelatine*
250 ml (1 cup) pomegranate juice
60 g monk fruit sweetener*
3 tablespoons rosewater
1 tablespoon tapioca flour* mixed
    with 1 tablespoon finely ground
    monk fruit sweetener,* to dust
    (optional)

* See Glossary

Grease a 25 cm x 15 cm Swiss roll tin and line the base and side with baking paper, cutting into the corners to fit.

Place 500 ml of water in a bowl and sprinkle over the gelatine. Set aside to soak for 5 minutes.

Meanwhile, combine the pomegranate juice and monk fruit sweetener in a small saucepan over medium–low heat and cook, stirring constantly, for 3–5 minutes. Add the gelatine mixture and whisk until smooth and the gelatine is dissolved, then mix in the rosewater. Pour into the prepared tin and refrigerate for 30 minutes to set.

Cut into bite-sized squares and dust lightly with the tapioca and monk fruit mixture (if desired). Serve.

Store your undusted Turkish delight in an airtight container in the fridge for up to 2 weeks (if dusted, the tapioca coating becomes pasty).

FROZEN YOGHURT

When I decided to give up dairy, one of the things I was concerned about was my love of ice cream and frozen yoghurt. I was a huge fan of those self-serve frozen yoghurt machines that some health food stores had – it was my all-time favourite treat. Luckily for me, many of those dairy frozen yoghurt machines have now been replaced with coconut yoghurt ones, and it's actually really easy to make at home also. You can top your frozen coconut yoghurt with any in-season fruit or, if you feel like going to a bit more effort, make these delicious fruit sauces to drizzle over.

500 g coconut yoghurt
2 tablespoons finely ground monk fruit sweetener*
  or xylitol*

RASPBERRY AND CHIA SAUCE
2 teaspoons chia seeds
250 g frozen raspberries, thawed
2 tablespoons finely ground monk fruit sweetener*
  or xylitol*

PASSIONFRUIT SAUCE
½ teaspoon powdered gelatine*
pulp of 3 passionfruit
3 tablespoons finely ground monk fruit sweetener*
  or xylitol*

* See Glossary

Combine the coconut yoghurt and sweetener in a bowl, then place in the freezer for 4 hours.

Place all the raspberry and chia sauce ingredients in a bowl. Stir, making sure the chia seeds are moistened with the juice from the raspberries. Place in a food processor and pulse two or three times to break up the berries. Transfer to the fridge to chill until ready to use.

Meanwhile, to make the passionfruit sauce, place 2 tablespoons of water in a bowl and sprinkle over the gelatine. Set aside to soak for 5 minutes. Combine the passionfruit pulp, sweetener and 2 tablespoons of water in a saucepan over medium–low heat and bring to a simmer. Remove from the heat, add the gelatine mixture and stir until the gelatine has completely dissolved. Allow to cool, then place in the fridge to chill until ready to use. Give the sauce a good mix before serving.

When ready to serve, scoop the frozen yoghurt into bowls and spoon over the passionfruit and raspberry and chia sauces.

CHOCOLATE AND COCONUT GUMMIES

My wife, Nic, is amazing at making anything with gelatine or collagen in it. We consume both every single day in either hot or cold preparations, as they provide so many essential building blocks for our bodies, from improving gut health to strengthening hair, nails, skin and digestion. Which is why I'm a massive fan of Nic's chocolate and coconut gummies. You can substitute any of your favourite flavours, as you wish.

olive oil, for greasing

CHOCOLATE LAYER
1 ½ tablespoons powdered gelatine*
300 ml coconut cream
1 tablespoon monk fruit sweetener*
2 tablespoons cacao powder
½ teaspoon ground cinnamon

COCONUT AND VANILLA LAYER
1 ½ tablespoons powdered gelatine*
300 ml coconut cream
2 tablespoons monk fruit sweetener*
¼ teaspoon vanilla powder or paste
5 drops of essential peppermint oil

* See Glossary

Grease a 35 cm x 25 cm Swiss roll tin with olive oil.

To make the chocolate layer, place 3 tablespoons of water in a bowl and sprinkle over the gelatine. Set aside to soak for 5 minutes.

Meanwhile, place the coconut cream, monk fruit sweetener, cacao powder and cinnamon in a small saucepan and whisk well. Place over medium–low heat and cook, stirring constantly, for 3–5 minutes until hot. Make sure you don't let the mixture boil. Add the gelatine mixture and whisk until incorporated. Pour the mixture through a fine sieve (to remove any small gelatine lumps) into the prepared tin and place in the refrigerator for 30 minutes to set.

Meanwhile, to start on the coconut and vanilla layer, place 3 tablespoons of water in a bowl and sprinkle over the gelatine. Set aside to soak for 5 minutes.

Place the coconut cream, monk fruit sweetener and vanilla in a small saucepan and whisk well. Place over medium–low heat and cook, stirring constantly, for 3–5 minutes until hot. Don't let the mixture boil. Add the gelatine mixture and peppermint oil and whisk until incorporated and smooth. Allow to cool for 10 minutes in the pan. Make sure the mixture doesn't set – it needs to be liquid when pouring into the tin.

Carefully pour the cooled coconut and vanilla mixture through a fine sieve into the tin to completely cover the chocolate layer, then return to the refrigerator for 1 hour to set.

Once the slab is set, turn out onto a chopping board. Cut into bite-sized squares or into your desired shape and serve. The gummies will keep in an airtight container or jar in the fridge for up to 2 weeks.

AIOLI

MAKES 470 G

4 roasted garlic cloves
4 egg yolks
2 teaspoons Dijon mustard
2 teaspoons apple cider vinegar
2 tablespoons lemon juice
420 ml (1 ⅔ cups) olive oil
sea salt and freshly ground black pepper

Place the garlic, egg yolks, mustard, vinegar, lemon juice, oil and a pinch of salt in a glass jug or jar and blend with a hand-held blender until smooth and creamy. (Alternatively, place the garlic, egg yolks, mustard, vinegar, lemon juice and a pinch of salt in the bowl of a food processor and process until combined. With the motor running, pour in the oil in a thin stream and process until thick and creamy.)

Season with salt and pepper to taste. Store in a sealed glass jar in the fridge for up to 5 days.

BEEF BONE BROTH

MAKES 3.5–4 LITRES

about 2 kg beef knuckle and marrow bones
1 calf foot, chopped into pieces (optional)
3 tablespoons apple cider vinegar
1.5 kg meaty beef rib or neck bones
3 onions, roughly chopped
3 carrots, roughly chopped
3 celery stalks, roughly chopped
2 leeks, white part only, roughly chopped
3 thyme sprigs
2 bay leaves
1 teaspoon black peppercorns, crushed
1 garlic bulb, halved horizontally
2 large handfuls of flat-leaf parsley stalks

Place the knuckle and marrow bones and calf foot (if using) in a stockpot, add the vinegar and pour in 5 litres of cold water, or enough to cover. Set aside for 1 hour to help draw out the nutrients from the bones. Remove the bones from the water, reserving the water.

Preheat the oven to 180°C (160°C fan-forced).

Place the knuckle and marrow bones, calf foot (if using) and meaty bones in a few large roasting tins and roast in the oven for 30–40 minutes until well browned. Return all the bones to the pot and add the vegetables.

Pour the fat from the roasting tins into a saucepan and add 1 litre of the reserved water, then place over high heat and bring to a simmer, stirring with a wooden spoon to loosen any coagulated juices. Add this liquid to the bones and vegetables. If necessary, add the remaining reserved water to the pot to just cover the bones – the liquid should come no higher than 2 cm below the rim of the pot, as the volume will increase slightly during cooking.

Bring the broth to the boil, skimming off the scum that rises to the top. Reduce the heat to low and add the thyme, bay leaves, peppercorns and garlic. Simmer for 12–24 hours. Just before finishing, add the parsley and simmer for 10 minutes. Strain into a large container, cover and refrigerate overnight.

The next day, remove the congealed fat that has risen to the top and reserve it for cooking; it will keep in the fridge for up to 1 week or in the freezer for up to 3 months. Transfer the thick and gelatinous broth to smaller airtight containers and place in the fridge or, for long-term storage, the freezer. The broth can be stored in the fridge for 3–4 days or freezer for up to 3 months.

BROCCOLI AND CAULIFLOWER RICE

SERVES 4–6

1 head of broccoli (about 300 g), florets and stalk roughly chopped
½ head of cauliflower (about 500 g), florets and stalk roughly chopped
2 tablespoons coconut oil
sea salt and freshly ground black pepper

Place the broccoli and cauliflower in a food processor and pulse into tiny pieces that look like rice.

Melt the coconut oil in a large frying pan over medium heat. Add the broccoli and cauliflower and cook, stirring occasionally, for 4–6 minutes until softened. Season with salt and pepper. The rice is best eaten straight away, but can be stored in an airtight container in the fridge for up to 4 days.

BROWN CHICKEN BONE BROTH

MAKES 4 LITRES

2.5 kg bony chicken parts (such as necks, breastbones and wings)
2–4 chicken feet
2 tablespoons apple cider vinegar
1 large onion, roughly chopped
2 carrots, roughly chopped
3 celery stalks, roughly chopped
1 leek, white part only, roughly chopped
1 garlic bulb, broken into cloves
1 tablespoon black peppercorns, lightly crushed
2 large handfuls of flat-leaf parsley stalks
2 fresh bay leaves

Preheat the oven to 200°C (180°C fan-forced).

Place the chicken bones and feet in a couple of large roasting tins and roast for 30–40 minutes until well browned.

Place the roasted chicken bones and feet in a stockpot. Add 5 litres of cold water, the vinegar, onion, carrot, celery, leek, garlic and peppercorns. Place over medium–high heat and bring to the boil, skimming off the scum that forms on the surface. Reduce the heat to low and simmer for 6–12 hours. The longer you cook the broth the more the flavour develops.

Allow the broth to cool slightly, then strain through a fine sieve into a large storage container. Cover and cool in the fridge. Once cool, remove the congealed fat that has risen to the top. It is a fantastic, stable cooking fat, and can be stored in a glass container in the fridge for up to 2 weeks and used for frying and sautéing. Transfer the gelatinous broth to smaller airtight containers and store in the fridge for up to 4 days or in the freezer for up to 3 months.

CAULIFLOWER RICE

SERVES 4

1 head of cauliflower, florets and stalks roughly chopped
2 tablespoons coconut oil
sea salt and freshly ground black pepper

Place the cauliflower in a food processor and pulse into tiny pieces that look like rice. Melt the coconut oil in a large frying pan over medium heat. Add the cauliflower and cook for 4–6 minutes until softened. Season with salt and pepper. The rice is best eaten straight away, but can be stored in an airtight container in the fridge for up to 4 days.

CHICKEN BONE BROTH

MAKES 3.5 LITRES

1–1.5 kg bony chicken parts (I like to use necks, backs, breastbones and wings)
2–4 chicken feet (optional)
2 tablespoons apple cider vinegar
1 large onion, roughly chopped
2 carrots, roughly chopped
3 celery stalks, roughly chopped
2 leeks, white part only, roughly chopped
1 garlic bulb, halved horizontally
1 tablespoon black peppercorns, lightly crushed
2 fresh bay leaves
2 large handfuls of flat-leaf parsley stalks

Place all the ingredients in a stockpot, add 5 litres of cold water and let stand for 1 hour to help draw out the nutrients from the bones.

Place the pot over medium–high heat and bring to the boil, skimming off the scum that forms on the surface. Reduce the heat to low and simmer for 12–24 hours. The longer you cook the broth the richer and more flavourful it will be. Strain the broth through a fine sieve, cover and refrigerate overnight.

The next day, remove the congealed fat that has risen to the top and reserve it for cooking; it will keep in an airtight glass container in the fridge for up to 1 week or in the freezer for up to 3 months. Transfer the broth to small airtight containers and refrigerate for up to 4 days or freeze for up to 3 months.

CHICKEN JUS

MAKES 650 ML

2 French shallots, chopped

6 thyme sprigs

300 ml dry white wine (such as sauvignon blanc)

1 tablespoon Dijon mustard

3 litres Brown Chicken Bone Broth (page 246)

1 ½ teaspoons tapioca flour* mixed with 1 tablespoon water (optional)

sea salt and freshly ground black pepper

* See Glossary

Place the shallot and thyme in a large, heavy-based saucepan and pour in the wine. Bring to the boil over medium–high heat and simmer until reduced by two-thirds.

Mix in the mustard, then pour in the broth and return to the boil. Reduce the heat to medium and simmer, occasionally skimming the scum that rises to the surface, until the jus has reduced by three-quarters to a sauce-like consistency. If the jus is still a little too thin, you can thicken it slightly by whisking in the tapioca mixture and simmering until it coats the back of a spoon.

Strain through a sieve and season with salt and pepper. Store in an airtight container in the fridge for up to 5 days or freeze for up to 3 months.

CRISPY PORK CRACKLING

SERVES 4

600 g pork rind, with at least 5 mm fat, scored

2 tablespoons melted coconut oil or good-quality animal fat*

2 ½ teaspoons sea salt

* See Glossary

Brush the pork rind with the coconut oil or fat, then rub with the salt and set aside at room temperature for 20 minutes.

Preheat the oven to 240°C (220°C fan-forced).

Place the pork rind on a wire rack in a roasting tin. Roast for 40 minutes, rotating the tin halfway through to prevent burning, until the pork crackling is golden and crisp. Keep a close eye on it in the final stages of cooking, as the edges may start to burn after 30 minutes. Cool for 5 minutes, then cut into bite-sized pieces with kitchen scissors. The crackling is best eaten the same day, but will keep in an airtight container in the fridge for up to 2 days.

NOTE Reserve the fat in the roasting tin and use it for cooking. Store the fat in an airtight container in the fridge for up to 2 weeks.

CRISPY SHALLOTS

MAKES ABOUT 3 TABLESPOONS

250 ml (1 cup) melted coconut oil or good-quality animal fat*

4–8 French shallots, finely sliced

*See Glossary

Melt the coconut oil or fat in a small saucepan over medium heat. Add the shallot and cook for 2–3 minutes until golden. Remove with a slotted spoon and drain on paper towel. (You can re-use the oil for sautéing vegetables or cooking meat, chicken or fish.) Store the crispy shallots in an airtight container in the pantry.

FERMENTED CHILLI SAMBAL

MAKES 1 X 1 LITRE JAR

800 g long red chillies
15 dried chillies
2 French shallots, chopped
5 garlic cloves, peeled
1 tablespoon finely grated ginger
½ teaspoon ground turmeric
1 tablespoon shrimp paste
2 teaspoons tamarind paste*
2 tablespoons coconut sugar
3 teaspoons sea salt
1 tablespoon fish sauce

* See Glossary

You will need a 1.5 litre preserving jar with an airlock lid for this recipe. Wash the jar and all the utensils you will be using in very hot water or run them through a hot rinse cycle in the dishwasher.

Place all the ingredients in a food processor and process until finely chopped. Pour in 125 ml of water and blend to a fine paste.

Spoon into the prepared jar, close the lid to seal, then wrap a tea towel around the side of the jar to block out the light; leave the airlock exposed. Store in a dark place with a temperature of 16–23°C for 7–10 days. (You can place the jar in an esky to maintain a more consistent temperature.)

After the chilli mixture has bubbled and brewed for about 1 week, set a fine sieve over a bowl. Tip in the chilli mixture and press down with a wooden spoon to extract as much sauce as possible (discard the leftover pulp). Pour the chilli sambal into a clean 1 litre jar and close the lid to seal. It will keep in the fridge for several months.

FLATBREADS

MAKES 7

170 g (1 ⅔ cups) almond meal
130 g tapioca flour*
½ teaspoon baking powder
125 ml (½ cup) coconut milk
3 eggs
½ teaspoon sea salt
coconut oil or good-quality animal fat,* for cooking

* See Glossary

Combine the almond meal, tapioca flour, baking powder, coconut milk, eggs, salt and 125 ml of water in a bowl.

Heat a small non-stick frying pan over medium heat. Add enough coconut oil or fat to coat the base of the pan, then pour in 80 ml of batter and swirl around. Cook for 2 minutes, or until mostly cooked through, then flip and cook for 1 minute, or until golden and crisp. Place the flatbread on a plate and repeat with the remaining mixture.

Store the flatbreads in an airtight container in the fridge for up to 1 week or freeze for up to 3 months.

FURIKAKE SEASONING

MAKES 30 G

2 nori* sheets, torn or snipped into 3 cm pieces
1 teaspoon sea salt
3 tablespoons bonito flakes*
a pinch of coconut sugar (optional)
1 teaspoon chilli flakes (optional)
1½ tablespoons sesame seeds, toasted

* See Glossary

Place the nori, salt and bonito flakes in a blender and pulse a few times to finely chop the nori. Mix in the sugar and chilli flakes (if using) and toasted sesame seeds. Store in an airtight container in the pantry for up to 3 months.

GARLIC CONFIT

MAKES 25 CLOVES

25 garlic cloves (about 100 g), peeled
250 ml (1 cup) melted coconut oil

Place the garlic and coconut oil in a saucepan over very low heat (do not allow the oil to boil). Gently poach for 1 hour, or until the garlic is beautifully soft.

Transfer the garlic and oil to a sterilised glass jar, seal and store in the fridge for up to 3 months.

GREEN GODDESS DRESSING

MAKES ABOUT 250 ML

½ avocado, roughly chopped
3 tablespoons coconut milk
3 tablespoons lemon juice
1 garlic clove, finely chopped
2 jarred salted anchovy fillets, rinsed and patted dry, finely chopped
2 large handfuls of flat-leaf parsley leaves, chopped
3 tablespoons chopped basil leaves
1 tablespoon chopped tarragon leaves
¼ teaspoon sea salt
125 ml (½ cup) extra-virgin olive oil

Place the avocado, coconut milk, lemon juice, garlic, anchovy, herbs and salt in a food processor and blitz until well combined. With the motor running, slowly pour in the oil and process until the dressing thickens and the herbs are finely chopped. Store in a glass jar in the fridge for up to 5 days.

HEMP MILK

MAKES 1 LITRE

130 g (1 cup) hemp seeds,* soaked in 500 ml (2 cups) water for 4 hours
1 litre filtered water

* See Glossary

Drain the hemp seeds and rinse well. Place in a blender, add the water and whiz for a few minutes until smooth.

Line a bowl with a large piece of muslin, allowing the muslin to hang over the edge of the bowl (alternatively, you can use a nut milk bag). Pour the hemp seed and water mixture into the lined bowl. Pick up the edges of the muslin and squeeze out all the milk.

Pour the hemp milk into a clean 1 litre glass bottle, then place in the fridge to chill.

Shake the bottle before use, as the milk will settle and separate over time. The hemp milk will keep in the fridge for up to 5 days.

HOT SAUCE

MAKES 500 ML

2 tablespoons coconut oil or good-quality animal fat*
1 onion, finely chopped
6 long red chillies, deseeded and chopped
2–3 habanero chillies, deseeded and chopped
4 garlic cloves, finely chopped
3 tomatoes, chopped
250 ml (1 cup) apple cider vinegar
2 teaspoons sea salt
1 tablespoon honey (optional)
2 tablespoons tamari or coconut aminos*

* See Glossary

Heat the coconut oil or fat in a large saucepan over medium heat. Add the onion, chilli, habanero chilli and garlic and cook for 5 minutes, or until softened. Reduce the heat to medium–low, then stir in the tomato, vinegar, salt, honey (if using) and tamari or coconut aminos. Simmer, stirring occasionally, until the tomato breaks down and the flavour develops, about 30 minutes. Allow to cool.

Transfer to a blender and whiz until smooth. Strain through a fine sieve, if desired, discarding the leftover pulp. Pour the hot sauce into clean glass jars with screw top lids and store in the fridge for up to 1 month.

JAPANESE MAYONNAISE

MAKES ABOUT 450 G

4 egg yolks
2 teaspoons Dijon mustard
1 ½ tablespoons apple cider vinegar
1 teaspoon tamari or coconut aminos*
¼ teaspoon garlic powder
400 ml olive or macadamia oil (or 200 ml of each)
sea salt and freshly ground black pepper

* See Glossary

Place the egg yolks, mustard, vinegar, tamari or coconut aminos, garlic powder, oil and a pinch of salt in a glass jug or jar and blend with a hand-held blender until smooth and creamy. (Alternatively, place the egg yolks, mustard, vinegar, tamari or coconut aminos, garlic powder and a pinch of salt in the bowl of a food processor and process until combined. With the motor running, slowly pour in the oil in a thin, steady stream and process until the mayonnaise is thick and creamy.)

Season with salt and pepper to taste. Store in a sealed glass jar in the fridge for up to 5 days.

KETO BREAD

MAKES 1 LOAF (10–12 SLICES)

160 g almond meal
40 g coconut flour
2 tablespoons psyllium husks*
2 teaspoons baking powder
1 teaspoon sea salt
450 g grated zucchini
3 garlic cloves, finely grated
1 ½ teaspoons finely chopped rosemary leaves
6 eggs, lightly beaten
120 ml extra-virgin olive oil

* See Glossary

Preheat the oven to 160°C (140°C fan-forced). Grease a 20 cm x 10 cm loaf tin and line the base and sides with baking paper, cutting into the corners to fit.

Combine the almond meal, coconut flour, psyllium husks, baking powder and salt in a large bowl. Add the zucchini, garlic, rosemary, egg and olive oil and stir well.

Spoon the mixture into the prepared tin and spread out evenly. Bake for 1 ½ hours, rotating the tin halfway through so the loaf cooks evenly. To check if the bread is cooked, insert a skewer in the centre; if it comes out clean, it's ready. Allow to cool a little in the tin before turning out onto a wire rack to cool completely.

Store in an airtight container in the fridge for up to 5 days or sliced in the freezer for up to 3 months.

KETO SOUR CREAM

MAKES ABOUT 500 G

155 g (1 cup) cashew nuts
about 1 litre filtered water
juice of 1 lemon, plus extra if desired
a pinch of sea salt

Soak the cashews in 750 ml of the filtered water for
2–4 hours. Drain and rinse well.

Place the cashews in a food processor or high-speed
blender, add the lemon juice, salt and 200 ml of the filtered
water and blend until smooth and creamy. Slowly pour
in more water if needed and process to a sour cream
consistency. Taste and add a little more lemon juice if
you like your sour cream to be tangier. Store in an airtight
container in the fridge for up to 5 days.

KIMCHI

MAKES 1 X 1 LITRE JAR

½ Chinese cabbage (wombok), cut into 5 cm pieces
2 tablespoons sea salt
4 garlic cloves, finely chopped
2 teaspoons finely grated ginger
1–2 tablespoons Korean chilli powder (gochugaru)*
    or chilli powder
2 tablespoons fish sauce
1½ tablespoons apple cider vinegar
1 tablespoon honey (optional)
3 spring onions, chopped
1 handful of coriander, roots, stalks and leaves,
    washed well and finely chopped
2 long red chillies, deseeded and finely sliced
filtered water (optional)

* See Glossary

Place the cabbage and salt in a large glass or stainless
steel bowl and mix well. Cover and set aside for 1 hour to
wilt the cabbage.

Meanwhile, place the garlic, ginger, chilli powder, fish
sauce, vinegar and honey (if using) in a bowl and mix well.

Rinse the cabbage thoroughly under cold water, drain well
and pat dry. Transfer the cabbage to a large bowl, add the
spring onion, coriander and chilli, then add the garlic and
ginger mixture and toss well.

You can serve the kimchi straight away or, for better results,
ferment it. To do this, you'll need a 1 litre preserving jar with
an airlock lid. Wash the jar and all utensils in very hot water
or run them through a hot rinse cycle in the dishwasher.

Fill the prepared jar with the kimchi, pressing down well with
a large spoon to remove any air pockets. The vegetables
should be completely submerged in the liquid; add some
filtered water if necessary. Seal with the lid and ferment for
2–3 days in a cool, dark place. The longer you leave the
kimchi to ferment the stronger the flavour will be. Chill
before eating. Once opened, the kimchi will keep in the
fridge for up to 3 weeks.

MAYONNAISE

MAKES ABOUT 500 G

4 egg yolks
2 teaspoons Dijon mustard
1 tablespoon apple cider vinegar
1 tablespoon lemon juice
400 ml olive or macadamia oil (or 200 ml of each)
sea salt and freshly ground black pepper

Place the egg yolks, mustard, vinegar, lemon juice, oil
and a pinch of salt in a glass jug or jar and blend with a
hand-held blender until smooth and creamy. (Alternatively,
place the egg yolks, mustard, vinegar, lemon juice and
a pinch of salt in the bowl of a food processor and process
until combined. With the motor running, slowly pour in the
oil in a thin stream and process until the mayonnaise is
thick and creamy.)

Season with salt and pepper to taste. Store in a sealed
glass jar in the fridge for up to 5 days.

PALEO MUESLI

40 g (¼ cup) cashew nuts (activated if possible),*
roughly chopped
40 g (¼ cup) macadamia nuts (activated if possible),*
roughly chopped
40 g (¼ cup) almonds (activated if possible),*
roughly chopped
25 g (¼ cup) walnuts (activated if possible),*
roughly chopped
2 tablespoons sunflower seeds (activated if possible)*
2 tablespoons pumpkin seeds (activated if possible)*
2 tablespoons flaxseeds
2 tablespoons currants (optional)
3 tablespoons coconut flakes

* See Glossary

Mix all the ingredients in a large bowl. Store in an airtight glass container in the pantry for up to 4 weeks.

PICKLED RED ONION

MAKES 300 G

1 red onion, cut into 12 wedges
125 ml (½ cup) red wine vinegar
2 fresh bay leaves
1 tablespoon honey
sea salt and freshly ground black pepper

Place the onion, vinegar, bay leaves and honey in a small saucepan and bring to a simmer over medium heat. Cover and cook for 1 minute, then remove from the heat and allow to cool completely. Season with salt and pepper. Store in an airtight glass jar in the fridge for up to 2 months.

PORK BONE BROTH

MAKES 3.5–4 LITRES

about 3.5 kg pork bones and knuckles
2 pork trotters (optional)
3 tablespoons apple cider vinegar
3 onions, roughly chopped
3 carrots, roughly chopped
3 celery stalks, roughly chopped
2 leeks, white part only, roughly chopped
3 thyme sprigs
2 fresh bay leaves
1 teaspoon black peppercorns, crushed
1 garlic bulb, halved horizontally
2 large handfuls of flat-leaf parsley stalks

Place the bones and knuckles and trotters (if using) in a stockpot, add the vinegar and pour in 5 litres of cold water, or enough to cover. Set aside for 1 hour to help draw out the nutrients from the bones. Remove the bones from the water, reserving the water.

Preheat the oven to 180°C (160°C fan-forced).

Transfer all the bones and knuckles and trotters (if using) to a few large roasting tins and roast for 30–40 minutes until browned. Return the bones to the pot and add the veggies.

Pour the fat from the roasting tins into a saucepan, add 1 litre of the reserved water, place over high heat and bring to a simmer, stirring with a wooden spoon to loosen any coagulated juices. Add this liquid to the bones and vegetables. If necessary, add the remaining reserved water to the pot to just cover the bones – the liquid should come no higher than 2 cm below the rim of the pot, as the volume will increase slightly during cooking.

Bring the broth to the boil, skimming off the scum that rises to the top. Reduce the heat to low and add the thyme, bay leaves, peppercorns and garlic. Simmer for 12–24 hours. Just before finishing, add the parsley and simmer for 10 minutes. Strain the broth into a large container, cover and place in the fridge overnight.

The next day, remove the congealed fat that has risen to the top and reserve it for cooking; it will keep in the fridge for up to 1 week or in the freezer for up to 3 months. Transfer the gelatinous broth to smaller airtight containers and store in the fridge for up to 4 days or in the freezer for up to 3 months.

PORK JUS

MAKES 650 ML

2 French shallots, chopped

6 thyme sprigs

300 ml dry white wine (such as sauvignon blanc)

1 tablespoon Dijon mustard

3 litres Pork Bone Broth (page 253)

1½ teaspoons tapioca flour* mixed with 1 tablespoon water (optional)

sea salt and freshly ground black pepper

* See Glossary

Place the shallot and thyme in a large, heavy-based saucepan and pour in the wine. Bring to the boil over medium–high heat and simmer until reduced by two-thirds. Mix in the mustard, then pour in the broth and return to the boil. Reduce the heat to medium and simmer, occasionally skimming the scum that rises to the surface, until the jus has reduced by three-quarters to a sauce-like consistency. If the jus is still a little too thin, you can thicken it slightly by whisking in the tapioca mixture and simmering until it coats the back of a spoon. Strain through a sieve and season with salt and pepper. Store in an airtight container in the fridge for up to 5 days or freeze for up to 3 months.

RED WINE JUS

MAKES ABOUT 600 ML

2 tablespoons coconut oil or good-quality animal fat*

100 g French shallots, sliced

2 garlic cloves, lightly crushed

6 thyme sprigs

3 tablespoons tomato paste

600 ml dry red wine (such as shiraz)

3 litres Beef Bone Broth (page 245)

sea salt and freshly ground black pepper

* See Glossary

Melt 1 tablespoon of the coconut oil or fat in a heavy-based saucepan over medium–high heat. Add the shallot and sauté for 5 minutes, or until lightly caramelised. Add the garlic, thyme and tomato paste and cook for 1 minute. Add the wine, bring to the boil and simmer until reduced by two-thirds.

Add the broth to the pan and return to the boil. Reduce the heat to medium and simmer, occasionally skimming the scum that rises to the surface, until the jus has reduced to about 600 ml and has a sauce-like consistency. Strain through a sieve and season with salt and pepper. Store in an airtight container in the fridge for up to 3 weeks or freeze for up to 3 months.

SMOKY BARBECUE SAUCE

MAKES 420 G

100 g tomato paste

3 tablespoons apple cider vinegar

1 tablespoon Dijon mustard

120 g honey

100 ml maple syrup

½ teaspoon smoked paprika

100 ml tamari or coconut aminos*

2 garlic cloves, finely chopped

1½ tablespoons liquid smoke (see Note) (optional)

a pinch of ground cloves

1 cinnamon stick

sea salt (optional)

* See Glossary

Place all the ingredients in a saucepan over medium heat, mix well and bring to a simmer. Reduce the heat to low and cook, stirring occasionally, for 10 minutes. Season with salt, if desired, and allow to cool. Remove the cinnamon stick and store in an airtight container in the fridge for up to 2 weeks.

NOTE Liquid smoke is a water-soluble liquid that forms from condensed smoke particles when chips from a hardwood (such as hickory) are burned. You can buy it from some supermarkets, delis, specialty food stores or online.

SPICED SEEDS

MAKES ABOUT 400 G

50 g (⅓ cup) flaxseeds
150 g (1 cup) pumpkin seeds (activated if possible)*
150 g (1¼ cups) sunflower seeds (activated if possible)*
1½ tablespoons sesame seeds
2 tablespoons coconut oil
2 teaspoons ground cumin
1 teaspoon ground coriander
3 teaspoons ground turmeric
a pinch of cayenne pepper
1 teaspoon honey (optional)
2 teaspoons tamari or coconut aminos*
¼ teaspoon fine sea salt

* See Glossary

Place the flaxseeds in a bowl, pour over enough water to cover by at least 2 cm and leave for 30 minutes. Preheat the oven to 160°C (140°C fan-forced). Line a large baking tray with baking paper.

Drain the flaxseeds (they will have a gelatinous texture) and place in a large bowl. Stir in the remaining ingredients. Spread over the tray and bake for 20–25 minutes until dry. Store in an airtight container in the pantry for up to 1 month.

SRIRACHA CHILLI SAUCE

MAKES 625 ML

680 g long red chillies, deseeded and roughly chopped
8 garlic cloves, crushed
½ red capsicum, deseeded and chopped
80 ml (⅓ cup) apple cider vinegar
2 tablespoons coconut sugar
2 tablespoons fish sauce
sea salt

Pulse all the ingredients in a high-speed blender until smooth. Pour into a saucepan and bring to the boil over high heat, stirring occasionally. Reduce the heat to low and simmer, stirring now and then, for 5–10 minutes. Add more water to reach your desired consistency and season with salt to taste. Transfer to a jar and store in the fridge for up to 2 weeks.

TERIYAKI SAUCE

MAKES 200 ML

125 ml (½ cup) tamari or coconut aminos*
3 tablespoons coconut sugar
3 tablespoons honey
2 teaspoons finely grated garlic
1 teaspoon finely grated ginger
1½ teaspoons tapioca flour*

* See Glossary

Mix the tamari or coconut aminos, sugar, honey, garlic, ginger and 3 tablespoons of water in a small saucepan and place over medium heat. Bring to the boil, then reduce the heat to low and gently simmer for 5 minutes to dissolve the sugar and allow the flavours to develop.

Meanwhile, mix the tapioca flour and 1 tablespoon of water until smooth and combined.

Bring the tamari mixture to the boil, then pour in the tapioca mixture. Stir constantly until thickened and the sauce coats the back of the spoon. Remove from the heat. Allow to cool, then strain, discarding the ginger and garlic pulp. Store in an airtight glass jar in the fridge for up to 4 weeks.

TOMATO KETCHUP

MAKES 330 G

180 g tomato paste
1 tablespoon apple cider vinegar
1 teaspoon garlic powder
1 teaspoon onion powder
½ teaspoon ground cinnamon
¼ teaspoon freshly grated nutmeg
1 teaspoon honey (optional)
a pinch of ground cloves

Mix the tomato paste with 100 ml of water in a small saucepan. Place over medium heat and bring to a simmer (add more water if you prefer your sauce to be thinner). Remove from the heat and stir in the remaining ingredients until incorporated and smooth. Cool and store in an airtight glass jar in the fridge for up to 4 weeks.

TURMERIC KRAUT

MAKES 1 X 1 LITRE JAR

600 g cabbage (you can use green or red, or a mixture of the two)
200 g grated carrot
2 tablespoons finely chopped ginger
3 teaspoons ground turmeric
2 teaspoons caraway seeds
2 tablespoons fine sea salt

You will need a 1 litre preserving jar with an airlock lid for this recipe. Wash the jar and all the utensils you will be using in very hot water or run them through a hot rinse cycle in the dishwasher.

Remove the outer leaves of the cabbage. Choose an unblemished outer leaf, wash it well and set aside.

Shred the cabbage in a food processor or slice with a knife or mandoline.

Place the shredded cabbage, carrot, ginger, turmeric and caraway seeds in a glass or stainless steel bowl, then sprinkle over the salt. Mix well and massage with very clean hands (or you can wear gloves) for 10 minutes to release some liquid.

Using a large spoon, fill the prepared jar with the cabbage mixture, pressing down well to remove any air pockets and leaving 2 cm of room free at the top. The vegetables should be completely submerged in the liquid. Add more water, if necessary.

Take the clean reserved cabbage leaf, fold it up and place it on top of the cabbage mixture, then add a small glass weight (a shot glass is ideal) to keep everything submerged. Close the lid and wrap a tea towel around the jar to block out the light. Store in a dark place at 16–23°C for 12–14 days. (You can place the jar in an esky to maintain a more consistent temperature.) Different vegetables have different culturing times and the warmer it is the shorter the time needed. The longer you leave the jar the higher the level of good bacteria present. It's up to you how long you leave it for – you may prefer the tangier flavour that comes with extra fermenting time.

Chill before eating. Once opened, the kraut will last for up to 2 months in the fridge when kept submerged in the liquid. Unopened, it will keep for up to 9 months in the fridge. Reserve the brine and use it to make delicious dressings.

TYPHOON GARLIC

MAKES 90 G

150 g garlic cloves (about 50), peeled
400 ml melted coconut oil
sea salt

To make the typhoon garlic, place the garlic in a food processor and process until finely chopped. Don't over-process as it will turn to mush.

Combine the garlic and coconut oil in a saucepan over medium heat, bring to the boil and cook, stirring frequently, for 8–12 minutes until the garlic is lightly golden and crispy. (The garlic can burn very quickly so remove the pan from the heat as soon as it turns pale golden.) Remove the garlic with a slotted spoon and drain on paper towel. (You can re-use the oil for sautéing vegetables or cooking meat, chicken or fish.) Season the garlic well with salt.

Transfer the garlic and oil to a sterilised glass jar, seal and store in the fridge for up to 1 month.

GLOSSARY

Activated charcoal
Activated charcoal is made from slowly burnt wood, peat or coconut shells treated with oxygen. What is left is a charcoal that is highly porous and is able to adsorb or bind to toxins and odours and expel them from the body. The powder is tasteless and odourless.

Activated nuts and seeds
Nuts and seeds are a great source of healthy fats, but they contain phytic acid, which binds to minerals so that they can't be readily absorbed. Activating nuts and seeds lessens the phytates, making minerals easier to absorb. Activated nuts and seeds are available from health food stores. To make your own, simply soak the nuts in filtered water (12 hours for hard nuts, such as almonds; 4–6 hours for softer nuts, such as cashews and macadamias). Rinse the nuts, then spread out on a baking tray and place in a 50°C oven or dehydrator to dry out. This will take anywhere from 6 to 24 hours, depending on the temperature and the kind of nuts or seeds. Store in an airtight container in the pantry for up to 3 months.

Arrowroot
Arrowroot is a starch made from the roots of several tropical plants. In Australia, arrowroot and tapioca flour are considered the same, even though they are actually from different plants. It can be found at health food stores and some supermarkets. *See also* Tapioca Flour.

Bonito flakes
Bonito flakes are made from the bonito fish, which is like a small tuna. The fish is smoked, fermented, dried and shaved, and the end product looks similar to wood shavings. Bonito flakes are used to garnish Japanese dishes, to make sauces such as ponzu, soups such as miso and the Japanese stock, dashi. You can find bonito flakes in Asian grocers.

Coconut aminos
Made from coconut sap, coconut aminos is similar in flavour to a light soy sauce. Because it is free of both soy and gluten, it makes a great alternative to soy sauce and tamari. Coconut aminos is available at health food stores.

Coconut oil
Coconut oil is extracted from the meat of mature coconuts. It has a high smoke point, making it great for cooking at high temperatures. The viscosity of coconut oil changes depending on the temperature and ranges from liquid to solid. Although coconut oil is high in saturated fats, they are mainly medium-chain saturated fatty acids, which means the body can use them quickly and does not have to store them. Coconut oil is available from supermarkets and health food stores. Look for virgin cold-pressed varieties, as these have had the least amount of processing.

Collagen
Collagen is a great way to increase your protein intake and ensure that your body is getting all the essential amino acids it needs for a healthy gut, strong hair and nails and healthy skin. You can buy it from health food stores and it can be added to desserts as well as hot dishes and smoothies.

Dashi
Dashi is a Japanese broth, which is made from kombu (a type of seaweed) and bonito (a type of fish). It adds a deep, umami flavour to dishes and is available from Asian grocers. Make sure you look for dashi with no nasties, such as MSG, added.

Diatomaceous earth
A powdered supplement made from a naturally occurring rock that contains fossilised algae, diatomaceous earth may help to support digestion, improve bone health, and promote healthy skin and hair. It can be added to drinks and smoothies and is available from health food stores.

Dulse flakes
Made from a type of red seaweed that has been dried, dulse flakes are rich in many vitamins and minerals, such as iron. They have a rich, salty, nutty flavour and are great sprinkled over soups and stews. They are available from Asian grocers and health food stores.

Gelatine

Gelatine is the cooked form of collagen, which is a protein found in bones, skin and connective tissue. I always choose gelatine sourced from organic, grass-fed beef, such as Great Lakes Gelatin Company. Vegetarian substitutes for gelatine include agar agar and carrageen, which are made from two different types of seaweed. Sometimes these aren't as strong as regular gelatine, so you may need to increase the quantity. Some kosher gelatines are also vegan. You can buy gelatine made from organic, grass-fed beef, agar agar and carrageen from health food stores or online.

Ghee

While I avoid dairy, ghee is a form of clarified butter that has had the milk solids removed, creating a pure fat with a high smoking point. It is good for cooking curries and is available from health food stores and some supermarkets. Always look for ghee made with butter from grass-fed cows.

Good-quality animal fat

I use either coconut oil or good-quality animal fats for cooking as they have high smoke points (meaning they do not oxidise at high temperatures). Some of my favourite animal fats to use are lard (pork fat), tallow (rendered beef fat), rendered chicken fat and duck fat. These may be hard to find – ask at your local butcher or meat supplier, look online for meat suppliers who sell them or make your own when making bone broths.

Hemp

Hemp is a wonderful source of nutrition. The seeds are rich in protein, fibre and healthy fats in the form of omega-3 fatty acids, and they can be used in so many ways – sprinkled over soups, added to baked goods or blended into smoothies. Hemp oil is made from cold-pressing hemp seeds, and it is rich in essential fatty acids and great for using in dressings or to drizzle over finished dishes. Both hemp seeds and oil are available from health food stores.

Jarred fish

I buy preserved fish – such as tuna, salmon, mackerel and sardines – in jars rather than cans, due to the presence of Bisphenol A (BPA) in many cans. BPA is a toxic chemical that can interfere with our hormonal system. You can find jarred fish at specialty food stores and supermarkets.

Kombu

Kombu is a high-protein sea vegetable that is rich in calcium, iron, iodine and dietary fibre. It is salty and savoury and plays an important role in Japanese cuisine. Kombu can be used in a similar way to bay leaves – add it to a stew or curry for a flavour boost and remove it after cooking. Kombu can be found in Asian grocers and is mainly sold dried or pickled in vinegar. Dried kombu is often covered with a white powder from natural salts and starch. It is harmless but can easily be removed with a damp cloth.

Korean chilli powder (gochugaru)

Korean chilli powder is made from thin red chillies that are dried in the sun and ground. It has smoky, fruity sweet notes, with a hot kick, and is used to make classic Korean dishes such as kimchi and bulgogi. It is also great for stir-fries, dipping sauces and meat marinades. You can find Korean chilli powder in Asian grocers.

Matcha powder

Made by grinding green tea leaves into a fine powder, matcha is rich in antioxidants and can be used in smoothies, treats and even salad dressings. It is available from health food stores and Asian grocers.

MCT oil

MCT stands for medium-chain triglycerides, a special type of saturated fatty acid that is easily digested to provide fast, sustained energy. MCT oil is believed to improve cognitive function and help maintain a healthy body weight. It's also great for balancing hormones, regulating blood sugar and supporting gut health, and it has antibacterial and antifungal properties.

If trying MCT oil for the first time, take 1 teaspoon, then, over the course of a few weeks, gradually add ½ teaspoon at a time every week or so. MCT oil on an empty stomach can cause nausea, so it's best to have it with food. If you are experiencing GI distress or diarrhoea, cut the dosage back.

Miso

Miso paste is made from fermented soybeans. It has a salty taste, buttery texture and unique nutritional profile that make it a versatile condiment for a host of different recipes, and a foundation for traditional miso soup. Miso paste ranges in colour from white to brown – the darker the colouring, the more robust the flavour and saltiness.

Nori

Nori is a dark green, paper-like, toasted seaweed used for most kinds of sushi and other Japanese dishes. Nori provides an abundance of essential nutrients and is rich in vitamins, iron, minerals, amino acids, omega-3 and omega-6, and antioxidants. Nori sheets are commonly used to roll sushi, but they can also be added to salads and soups, as well as fish, meat and vegetable dishes. You can buy nori sheets from Asian grocers and most supermarkets.

Nutritional yeast

Nutritional yeast is a source of complete protein and vitamins, in particular B-complex vitamins. It contains thiamine, folates, niacin, selenium, zinc and riboflavin, making it a highly nutritious addition to your diet.

Pomegranate molasses

Pomegranate molasses is a thick, tangy and glossy reduction of pomegranate juice that is rich in antioxidants. Pomegranate molasses is used in Middle Eastern countries for glazing meat and chicken before roasting, and in sauces, salad dressings and marinades. You can buy it from Middle Eastern grocers and some supermarkets.

Psyllium husks

Psyllium, also known as ispaghula, is a gluten-free, soluble fibre produced from the Plantago ovata plant, native to India and Pakistan. Psyllium is an indigestible dietary fibre and is primarily used to maintain intestinal health, as the high fibre content absorbs excess liquid in the gut. When exposed to liquids, the husks swell up to create a gel. It is therefore important to drink plenty of fluids when consuming psyllium. Psyllium products can be found at health food stores and some supermarkets.

Salt

I use sea salt or Himalayan salt in my cooking, as they are less processed than table salt, contain more minerals and have a lovely crunchy texture. Himalayan salt is light pink in colour due to the presence of a number of different minerals, including iron, magnesium, calcium and copper. You can buy sea salt and Himalayan salt at supermarkets and health food stores.

Shichimi togarashi

Shichimi togarashi literally means 'seven flavour chilli pepper' and is one of the most popular condiments on Japanese tables. As the name suggests, this spice mixture is made from seven ingredients, typically red chilli, Japanese (sansho) peppers, orange peel, black and white sesame seeds, ginger and seaweed. The chillies aside, the ingredients vary, and if you are lucky you may come across a Japanese vendor offering a custom blend.

Sumac

Sumac is a spice made from red sumac berries that have been dried and crushed. It has antimicrobial properties and a tangy, lemony flavour, which makes it ideal for pairing with seafood. It's also delicious in salad dressings. You can buy it from Middle Eastern grocers, delis and some supermarkets.

SWEETENERS

- Erythritol
Erythritol is a naturally-derived sugar substitute, produced by a fermentation process, which looks and tastes very much like sugar, yet has almost no calories. It comes in granulated and powdered forms. Erythritol has been used in Japan since 1990 in sweets, chocolate, yoghurt, fillings, jellies, jams and beverages. Erythritol is classified as a sugar alcohol. Sugar alcohols, also called polyols, are sugar substitutes that are either extracted from plants or manufactured from starches. You can buy it online or from health food stores.

- Monk fruit sweetener
Monk fruit is a small, green gourd that resembles a melon. It is grown in Southeast Asia. The fruit was first used by Buddhist monks in the 13th century, hence the fruit's unusual name. Monk fruit sweeteners are made from the fruit's extract. They may be blended with dextrose or other ingredients to balance sweetness. Monk fruit extract is 150–200 times sweeter than sugar. The extract contains zero calories and zero carbohydrates. Monk fruit sweetener can be found online and in health food stores.

- Stevia
Native to South America, stevia grows into a shrub with naturally sweet leaves. The sweet extraction has no calories and is over 100 times sweeter than cane sugar. Stevia leaves have been used by the people of Brazil and Paraguay for hundreds of years as a means of sweetening food. Stevia is also believed to provide relief from skin irritations. You can find stevia in most supermarkets.

- Xylitol
Xylitol is a sugar alcohol found in fruits and vegetables. It is low in carbohydrates and slowly absorbed, so has a minimal effect on blood sugar, making it useful for people wishing to avoid sugar. You can find granulated xylitol in health food stores and some supermarkets.

Tapioca flour
Tapioca flour is made by grinding up the dried root of the manioc (also known as cassava) plant. It can be used to thicken dishes or in gluten-free baking. You can find tapioca flour at health food stores and some supermarkets. *See also* Arrowroot.

Tobiko
Also known as flying fish roe, tobiko is commonly used in Japanese cuisine. The fish eggs are usually an orange–red colour and have a mild flavour. I love sprinkling tobiko across a whole range of dishes as a beautiful garnish. Tobiko is available from some Asian grocers, specialty food stores and fish mongers.

Wakame
Wakame is an edible seaweed used in Japanese, Korean and Chinese cuisine. It's great in soups, salads and stir-fries. Wakame contains iron, magnesium, iodine, calcium and lignans. You can find it in Asian grocers and some supermarkets.

Yuzu juice
Yuzu is a Japanese citrus fruit that has an extraordinary spicy citrus flavour, somewhere between a lemon and a lime. Yuzu juice is very high in vitamin C and is great in cocktails, dressings, dips and sashimi dishes. You can buy yuzu juice from Asian grocers.

Za'atar
Za'atar is a Middle Eastern spice mix that is used to flavour meats, seafood, eggs, soups, vegetables and poultry. Za'atar contains thyme, sumac, sesame seeds, oregano, marjoram and salt. You can buy it from Middle Eastern grocers, delis and some supermarkets.

CONVERSION CHARTS

Measuring cups and spoons may vary slightly from one country to another, but the difference is generally not enough to affect a recipe. All cup and spoon measures are level.

One Australian metric measuring cup holds 250 ml (8 fl oz), one Australian metric tablespoon holds 20 ml (4 teaspoons) and one Australian metric teaspoon holds 5 ml. North America, New Zealand and the UK use a 15 ml (3-teaspoon) tablespoon.

LENGTH

METRIC	IMPERIAL
3 mm	⅛ inch
6 mm	¼ inch
1 cm	½ inch
2.5 cm	1 inch
5 cm	2 inches
18 cm	7 inches
20 cm	8 inches
23 cm	9 inches
25 cm	10 inches
30 cm	12 inches

LIQUID MEASURES

ONE AMERICAN PINT	ONE IMPERIAL PINT
500 ml (16 fl oz)	600 ml (20 fl oz)

CUP	METRIC	IMPERIAL
⅛ cup	30 ml	1 fl oz
¼ cup	60 ml	2 fl oz
⅓ cup	80 ml	2½ fl oz
½ cup	125 ml	4 fl oz
⅔ cup	160 ml	5 fl oz
¾ cup	180 ml	6 fl oz
1 cup	250 ml	8 fl oz
2 cups	500 ml	16 fl oz
2¼ cups	560 ml	20 fl oz
4 cups	1 litre	32 fl oz

DRY MEASURES

The most accurate way to measure dry ingredients is to weigh them. However, if using a cup, add the ingredient loosely to the cup and level with a knife; don't compact the ingredient unless the recipe requests 'firmly packed'.

METRIC	IMPERIAL
15 g	½ oz
30 g	1 oz
60 g	2 oz
125 g	4 oz (¼ lb)
185 g	6 oz
250 g	8 oz (½ lb)
375 g	12 oz (¾ lb)
500 g	16 oz (1 lb)
1 kg	32 oz (2 lb)

OVEN TEMPERATURES

CELSIUS	FAHRENHEIT
100°C	200°F
120°C	250°F
150°C	300°F
160°C	325°F
180°C	350°F
200°C	400°F
220°C	425°F

CELSIUS	GAS MARK
110°C	¼
130°C	½
140°C	1
150°C	2
170°C	3
180°C	4
190°C	5
200°C	6
220°C	7
230°C	8
240°C	9
250°C	10

ENDNOTES

1. Wheless JW. History of the ketogenic diet. *Epilepsia*. 2008;49 Suppl 8:3–5.

2. Montgomery MK, Turner N. Mitochondrial dysfunction and insulin resistance: An update. *Endocrine Connections*. 2015;4(1):R1–R15.

3. Fery F, Melot C, Balasse EO. Glucose fluxes and oxidation after an oral glucose load in patients with non-insulin-dependent diabetes mellitus of variable severity. *Metabolism*. 1993;42(4):522–30.

4. Singla P, Bardoloi A, Parkash AA. Metabolic effects of obesity: A review. *World Journal of Diabetes*. 2010;1(3):76–88.

5. van den Brink W, van Bilsen J, Salic K, Hoevenaars FMP, Verschuren L, Kleemann R, Bouwman J, Ronnett GV, van Ommen B, Wopereis S. Current and future nutritional strategies to modulate inflammatory dynamics in metabolic disorders. *Frontiers in Nutrition*. 2019;6:129.

6. Gross EC, Lisicki M, Fischer D, Sandor PS, Schoenen J. The metabolic face of migraine – from pathophysiology to treatment. *Nature Reviews Neurology*. 2019;15:627–43.

7. Sam S. Adiposity and metabolic dysfunction in polycystic ovary syndrome. *Hormone Molecular Biology and Clinical Investigation*. 2015;21(2):107–16.

8. Seyfried TN, Flores RE, Poff AM, D'Agostino DP. Cancer as a metabolic disease: Implications for novel therapeutics. *Carcinogenesis*. 2014;35(3):515–27.

9. Ormazabal V, Nair S, Elfeky O, Aguayo C, Salomon C, Zuniga FA. Association between insulin resistance and the development of cardiovascular disease. *Cardiovascular Diabetology*. 2018;17:122.

10. Calsolaro V, Edison P. Alterations in glucose metabolism in Alzheimer's disease. *Recent Patents on Endocrine Metabolic & Immune Drug Discovery*. 2016;10(1):31–39.

11. Crofts C, Zinn C, Wheldon MC, Schofield GM. Insulin resistance: A unifying theory of chronic disease? *Diabesity*. 2015;1(4):34–43.

12. Yang H, Shan W, Zhu F, Wu J, Wang Q. Ketone bodies in neurological diseases: Focus on neuroprotection and underlying mechanisms. *Frontiers in Neurology*. 2019;10:585.

13. Kovacs Z, D'Agostino DP, Diamond D, Kindy MS, Rogers C, Ari C. Therapeutic potential of exogenous ketone supplement induced ketosis in the treatment of psychiatric disorders: Review of current literature. *Frontiers in Psychiatry*. 2019;10:363.

14. Gross, et al. *Nature Reviews Neurology*. 2019;15:627–43.

15. Mukherjee P, Augur ZM, Li M, Hill C, Greenwood B, Domin MA, Kondakci G, Narain NR, Kiebish MA, Bronson RT, Arismendi-Morillo G, Chinopoulos C, Seyfried TN. Therapeutic benefit of combining calorie-restricted ketogenic diet and glutamine targeting in late-stage experimental glioblastoma. *Communications Biology*. 2019;2:200.

16. Cunnane S, Nugent S, Roy M, Courchesne-Loyer A, Croteau E, Tremblay S, Castellano A, Pifferi F, Bocti C, Paquet N, Begdouri H, Bentourkia M, Turcotte E, Allard M, Barberger-Gateau P, Fulop T, Rapoport SI. Brain fuel metabolism, aging, and Alzheimer's disease. *Nutrition*. 2011;27:3–20.

17. Cunnane, et al. *Nutrition*. 2011;27:3–20.

18. Mosconi L. Glucose metabolism in normal aging and Alzheimer's disease: Methodological and physiological considerations for PET studies. *Clinical and Translational Imaging*. 2013;1(4):10.

19. Kovacs, et al. *Frontiers in Psychiatry*. 2019;10:363.

20. La Berge AF. How the ideology of low fat conquered America. *Journal of the History of Medicine and Allied Sciences*. 2008;63(2):139–77.

21. Temple NJ. Fat, sugar, whole grains and heart disease: 50 years of confusion. *Nutrients*. 2018;10(1):39.

22. Malhotra A. Saturated fat is not the major issue. *BMJ*. 2013;347:f6340.

23. Bhanpuri NH, Hallberg SJ, Williams PT, McKenzie AL, Ballard KD, Campbell WW, McCarter JP, Phinney SD, Volek JS. Cardiovascular disease risk factor responses to a type 2 diabetes care model including nutritional ketosis induced by sustained carbohydrate restriction at 1 year: An open label, non-randomized, controlled study. *Cardiovascular Diabetology*. 2018;17:56.

24. Wheless J. History of the ketogenic diet. *Epilepsia*. 2008;49:s8.

25. Ruiz Herrero J, Canedo Villarroya E, Garcia Penas JJ, Garcia Alcolea B, Gomez Fernandez, B, Puerta Macfarland LA, Pedro Giner C. Safety and effectiveness of the prolonged treatment of children with a ketogenic diet. *Nutrients*. 2020;12(2):306.

26. Paoli A, Mancin L, Giacona MC, Bianco A, Caprio M. Effects of a ketogenic diet in overweight women with polycystic ovary syndrome. *Journal of Translational Medicine*. 2020;18(1):104.

THANK YOU

A mountain of gratitude to my glorious family, especially my wonderful wife, Nic, and my two amazing daughters, Indii and Chilli. You three angels are a constant source of pure inspiration and happiness, and it is a humbling honour to walk beside you all throughout this life. Thank you for being your bright, fun-loving, authentic and unconditionally loving selves.

To the absolute wonder twins, Monica and Jacinta Cannataci, you both add your own magic essence to everything we create together, and this book just wouldn't be the same without your input. Thank you both for working so graciously and tirelessly, and for all that you do!

To the incredible photography and styling team of William Meppem, Rob Palmer and Lucy Tweed. You all bring a unique sense of beauty that never ceases to be exceptionally pleasing, and I'm endlessly thankful to you all.

To Kristi Storoschuk, thank you so much for helping get this book to where it is now. So many people will benefit greatly from all your hard work and knowledge.

To Mary Small, thank you for passionately orchestrating the path that allows so much goodness to come to life. It is a pleasure to work with you both, always!

Thanks to Jane Winning, for making sure everything is as it should be. It is a joy to have you crossing the T's and dotting the I's.

To Clare Keighery, thanks for being the best publicist any author could wish to work with.

To Megan Johnston, thank you for your careful and thorough editing.

To Madeleine Kane, thank you for creating such a gorgeous design for the book.

A very warm thank you to my sweet mum, Joy. Among many things, you passed on your love of cooking and there's no doubt that I wouldn't be where I am without you.

I also wish to express a huge thank you to my teachers, peers, mentors and friends, who are all genuinely working towards creating a healthier world and who are all in their own right true forces for good: Nora Gedgaudas and Lisa Collins, Trevor Hendy, Rudy Eckhardt, Dr Pete Bablis, Dr David Perlmutter, Dr Alessio Fasano, Dr Kelly Brogan, Dr William Davis, Dr Joseph Mercola, Helen Padarin, Dr Natasha Campbell-McBride, Dr Frank Lipman, Dr Libby, Prof. Tim Noakes, Pete Melov and Prof. Martha Herbert, to name a few.

INDEX

A PLUM BOOK

First published in 2020 by
Pan Macmillan Australia Pty Limited
Level 25, 1 Market Street,
Sydney, NSW, Australia 2000

Level 3, 112 Wellington Parade,
East Melbourne, Victoria, Australia 3002

Design and typesetting by Madeleine Kane
Editing by Megan Johnston
Index by Helena Holmgren
Photography by William Meppem, with additional photography
by Steve Brown and Mark Roper
Prop and food styling by Lucy Tweed, with additional styling by Deb Kaloper
Food preparation by Jacinta and Monica Cannataci
Colour reproduction by Splitting Image Colour Studio
Printed and bound in China by 1010 Printing International Limited

A CIP catalogue record for this book is available from the National Library of Australia.

10 9 8 7 6 5 4 3 2 1